Inspirational true

Becoming Human
being human®

ALI-SALAAM

An American Muslim Perspective

© Copyright 2002 Ali-Salaam. All rights reserved Al Andalus Turst Media and Publications.

No part of this publication may be reproduced, stored in a retrieval system, or transmitted, in any form or by any means, electronic, mechanical, photocopying, recording, or otherwise, without the written prior permission of the author.

Al Andalus Trust Media & Publications, U.S.A.
in cooperation with
Trafford Publishing, Canada

contact the author at: requests@becominghuman.net
info@alisalaam.com

Al Andalus Trust

Media & Publications

National Library of Canada Cataloguing in Publication Data

Ali-Salaam
    Becoming human, being human / Ali-Salaam.
ISBN 1-55395-015-1
    I. Title.
BJ1597.A44 2002   170'.44   C2002-904056-6

10   9   8   7   6   5

AMAZON.COM
readers give
Ali-Salaam
★★★★★

A Must Read

An eminently poignant essay on humanity at a most auspicious moment in our history. A must read for the seeker of truth.
M. Blumsfeld, Sydney, Australia

Dynamically Inspirational

I have been disillusioned by all the war and negative events in America and abroad here a patriotic American and a Muslim has shown me that within every crisis one can find joy and hope.
Michael, Warwick, RI

Masterpiece

Poignant, timely and a beautiful message articulated masterfully. I enjoyed the works of Mark Victor Hansen, Dr. Wayne Dyer and Richard Bach. Ali-Salaam has joined the company of visionary leadership we need for the new millennium.
James Harold Smith, Austin, Texas

Visionary!

The divide of east and west evaporates in the breadth of Ali-Salaam's "Becoming Human; Being Human". A world not divided by linguistic archetypes, religous dogma, but a world uplifted by the common understanding of the inalienable rights of all people... I anticipate this book to make it to the Best Seller's List! *C. Rourke, Boston, Ma*

A Deserving Award Winner

... a dynamic, gifted and sensitive writer. I lived each breath of the people whose true stories changed my life. I loved the story of the "9-11 Hero". *Nancy B. Chicago, IL.*

About the Author

Ali-Salaam recalls as a schoolboy walking the 'Freedom Trail', and standing in front of the Old Massachusetts State House. He stood exactly on the spot where Crispus Attucks an African and the first matyr for the cause of colonialists' liberty was slain. The awe he felt as a boy walking the footpath haunts him four decades later; Ali-Salaam states:

"Whose heart can find rest until the founding ideals of our nation are deemed as an inextinguishable right for all of humankind?"

On a scale of 1 to 10; it deserves a 10

Becoming Human; Being Human by Ali-Salaam is an American Muslim perspective on today's issues. The book is a compilation of quotes and stories that examines the worlds' problems and crises through the eyes of the humans living through them. These disasters range from the 9/11 terrorist attack on the World Trade Center, and the civil wars and hunger that plague Africa, to the Palestinian /Israeli conflict. This book although non-fiction reads like a collection of well-told tales, some filled with the horror of war and conquest, others vibrating with the courage of the human spirit. I did find this book to be not just a wonderful collection of tales but also a marvelous philosophy of life. It did deserve *The Rising Star Award* from The Literary Guild. I highly recommend it.

Judith Woolcock Colombo,
Author of The Fablesinger & Night Crimes

Coming Soon,

Becoming Human; Being Human
Soul of the Survivors

A Story for Children of All Ages
First Light of the Moon

An Inspirational Journey in Devotion
Forty Days Beyond Time

from the records
Ali-Salaam

Becoming Human; Being Human Seminar Series

Ali-Salaam is a speaker with a gift of presence. He combines profound thought with an appealing language that draws his listeners to accept his message. Ali commands an almost reverent posture from his audience because he says what others know to be true deep inside them; fortunately, Ali-Salaam knows when to insert a lighthearted anecdote or a whimsical phrase. His message is stimulating, pleasurable and life-changing.

EMMY HAGGER, LIEUTENANT GOVERNOR OF MARKETING
TOASTMASTERS INTERNATIONAL

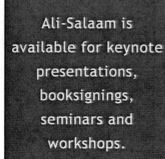

Ali-Salaam is available for keynote presentations, booksignings, seminars and workshops.

Learn more by visiting
www.ali-salaam.com

KEYNOTE PRESENTATION
inquiries can be sent to
info@ali-salaam.com

the X factor

Leadership for the New Millenium

Dedication

I've dedicated this work in the name of the Supreme Divinity; and to my mother who nobly endured the suffering of cancer with little relief, to my sister a courageous cancer survivor and my wife, who while faced with the threat of cancer to her own life kept me focused and inspired to complete this work, and believed in its value to mankind. I am eternally grateful to them.

In the name of the Infinite Sublime Divinity it is with humbleness and gratitude to my beloved parents, my children; dearest members of the human family who have been my loving and sincere teachers.

Thank you to Clara and John, who fostered me with genuine love, may the Supreme Sublime Divinity forever embrace your souls.

A Prayer for Humanity

Oh Immortal Sublime Divinity;
  We seek refuge in YOU from
  fear, miserliness and vanity.

Oh Immortal Sublime Divinity;
  We seek to release ourselves in
  the reality of Your existence.

Oh Immortal Sublime Divinity;
  We accept the authority and
  ability to do good and act just.

Oh Immortal Sublime Divinity;
  We seek Your protection from
  malice, despair and ignorance.

Oh Immortal Sublime Divinity;
  We seek liberation, freedom;
  and dignity for all.

  Ameen.

from the records, Ali-Salaam

The prose segments of this work were initially a letter to several world leaders including President George W. Bush, Prime Minister Ariel Sharon, Chairman Yasser Arafat, President Sayyid Mohammed Khatemi, Prime Minister Tony Blair and Prince Abdullah bin 'Abdul 'Aziz al-Saud.

At the insistence of friends and colleagues this work has been expanded and now includes true stories on being human.

Contents

Forward 12
Prologue 14
Sylvia 17
Becoming 38
Trapped In Iraq 43
Being 64
Rebuilding the Lion Mountain 67
A 9-11 Hero 80
Become Human 88
Children of the Prophets 90
A Matter of Conscience 104
The Universe 115
Two Prayers 120
Ta'ayush ~ Living Together 132
A Stand for Justice 140
Be Human 144
From Sea to Shining Sea 148
Being Human 189
Letter of Pope John Paul II 191
Decalogue of Assisi for Peace 193
An Echo from the Drum of War 196
Osama's Letter 197
Epilogue 202

Forward

In the heart of humanity is a wonder and knowingness of something that is intangible, intelligent and unmistakably alive. Throughout the records of our civilizations we have wrapped this infinite immortal existence in the expressions of cults, dogma, and religion.

Belief is the art of science and acknowledgment of Divinity, it is at the heart of our achieving truly moral societies. Whatever language or ritual we choose to express the reality of Divinity it is our cognizance of Divinity that binds humanity; even if the recognition of Divinity is to deny it's existence.

It is in acknowledgment of the Immortal Reality of Divinity who bestowed upon humanity the gift of reason that permits me to contribute this work in hopes that it will lead us to truly consider what is to be human.

Al Fatihah
(The Opening)

In the name of ALLAH,
Most Gracious, Most Merciful.
Praise be to ALLAH,
the Cherisher and Sustainer of the world;
Most Gracious, Most Merciful;
Master of the Day of Judgment.
Thee alone do we worship, and Thine aid we seek.
Show us the straight way, The way of those on whom
Thou hast bestowed Thy Grace,
those whose (portion) is not wrath,
and who go not astray.

The Quran, the Book of Wisdom

Chapter 1

Prologue

We are living at a time in our collective human experience that offers tremendous opportunities and challenges. Challenges that demands our world leaders and the common man to consider; what it is the true nature of humanity.

As we extinguish the lives of children in the womb, those children that survive are now ending their lives and others most violently. Children are abducted from their beds and are forced to endure the most tragic of experiences.

An unparalleled disregard for life and dignity surrounds us; and only the satisfaction of material desires and sensual stimulation seems to motivate our collective soul.

Humanity has reached a point of critical mass in which either we will recognize our noblest nature or succumb to the never ending cycle of conquest and destruction.

We can rationalize our reckless course in the guise of social systems, ideological supremacy and religious and / or political hegemony; or as a species we can rekindle the quest for understanding our magnanimous and aspiring spiritual nature.

We can want for others what we want for ourselves; we can do unto others as we would have done unto ourselves.

These inspirational ideals can only take root in our consciousness if we embrace our variance in culture, traditions, ethnicity; and transcend them by becoming and being human.

Our planet is poorly equipped for delight.
One must snatch gladness from the days that are.
In this life it's not difficult to die;
To make life is more difficult by far.
*Vladimir Mayakovsky,
from a poem called "Sergei Yessenin*

Sylvia

A Discovery

Sylvia's youthful face defied her fifty-three years. Deep wide-set almond eyes with the sparkle of youth were like two black jewels set in mahogany. Tall stature, square shoulders and a confident walk beguiled the young men at the office of the insurance company where she worked in Brockton, Massachusetts. As a member of the company's vast staff of accounting personnel, Sylvia was diligent, reliable and outgoing. She was quick with a smile and advice to those who sought her counsel. Sylvia's picturesque health deceived her and those who knew her.

One morning after her shower, Sylvia noticed that one of her breasts seemed different. It wasn't something she could explain but they just looked different from before. Maybe it was the shape, she could not be sure. She palpated it and it felt fine or at least there were no lumps. Hmmm, she pursed her narrow lips, tilted her head and stared at herself again in the mirror. They never seemed so asymmetrical. The reflection of the clock behind her told her that if she didn't get a move on she would miss the bus and be late for work. Hurriedly she dressed, grabbed her satchel and headed out the door. She walked her youngest daughter to the school bus stop before catching the Metro.

Sylvia sat on the bus casually looking through the morning paper, her thoughts drifted to her eldest son; as they so often did. The last time I saw him was sometime in late 1989 or early 1990 she recounted to herself. The diesel engine of the Metro bus roared as it rounded the turn on Perkins Avenue, the drive suddenly stopped short jolting all the passengers. The small white compact whisked past oblivious to the palpating hearts aboard the bus. Sylvia looked up from the morning newspaper;

"Umm, umm," she sighed, "some people.'"

Every so often the ads in the marquees above the seats change. She gave them a quick perusal and one in particular caught her attention. *'Over forty, have you had your annual mammogram,'* it read. Sylvia knew that she must and would.

"Humph" she sighed and inconspicuously looked down at her chest.

The Telephone Rings

It was Saturday morning, she had gotten up early and taken a short walk; the doctor said it was good for her chronic asthma. Following her typical routine she relaxed on the couch for a brief nap. The telephone jarred Sylvia from her repose. She reached for the telephone thinking it was Nadine or Harriet, one of her neighborhood friends. It was the hospital; they said she needed to come in on Monday. Sylvia hung up the phone.

Monday morning Sylvia called in late for work, after all the hospital wasn't far and she could get there rather quickly after her appointment by taking a cab, that will put a little squeeze on my budget she thought.

Sylvia took the bus home from the hospital.

Tuesday, Sylvia called in to work again; she would be having surgery this week and would need a leave of absence. Later that week, the doctors removed one of her breasts.

Weeks passed but eventually Sylvia returned to work where flowers, cheers, welcome backs and embraces were in abundance. She was not one to stand on ceremony and ordered everyone to get back to work; after all she had a lot of catching up to do. Her coworkers were delighted that the office matron had returned; but concerned whispers persisted at the water cooler, her eyes seemed to have lost a little sparkle they said.

Several weeks later the doctors removed Sylvia's other breast.

The northeast winds were chilly but that didn't prevent many people in the insurance accounting office from waiting outside the doors; others stood around their desks, today, Sylvia would return to work. "Here she is," someone shouted, more smiles, flowers and embraces. This time she did not direct everyone back to work; there was very little sparkle in her eyes, someone whispered.

Another said, "She looks pregnant."

"That's from the chemo you idiot," chided another.

"Shhh, she'll hear you; you jerks," whispered another.

She did hear them.

The winter holidays passed and things finally seemed to be getting back to normal thought Sylvia, or as normal as they could be. The truth was she was always very tired. Sylvia caught the Metro to work and settled into a window seat and began to flip through the morning paper. She hadn't heard from her eldest son in such a long time. She wondered how he was doing, didn't he have another daughter, umm-hmm; that's right, late this past summer or was it the summer before. She folded her newspaper and searched her satchel for a photocopy she had made from microfiche at the library.

After a few moments of shuffling through dozens of clippings, "Humph, here it is," she sighed audibly. Sylvia, quickly reread the birth announcement; August 17, 1988, that means she's a little over two years old now, she reflected. Sylvia had never seen her.

"Humph," she sighed again.

The Visitor's Promise

Winter passed into early spring. It was Saturday morning and Sylvia wanted to get up for a walk; she just needed a little more rest. Suddenly, there was an unfamiliar knock at the door;

"Andrea can you get that," she asked?

Andrea opened the door to find her big brother smiling down at her; she never knew when she would see him, but he always made her feel special. Andrea immediately demanded her rare but customary piggyback ride. Sylvia heard her youngest daughter's delighted squeals and laughter and wondered who it was.

"What's all that noise," she said, "Who is it Andrea?"

Now, the unfamiliar knock tapped with hesitation on her bedroom door.

"Come in," she said with anticipation.

The door opened and there stood her eldest son with the quiet smile, his little sister clinging and hanging on to the back of his neck.

"Okay, now Andrea, get down now and give your big brother a rest," she said. Andrea darted off to play.

Sylvia's eldest son looked at her with his bright deep intelligent eyes, our family's hallmark she mused to herself. He still looked like a teenager or no more than twenty-two or three, how old is he she thought, umm, that's right he's about thirty-five or so. Sylvia's son was shocked to see how old his mother looked. There is only sixteen or seventeen years between us he recalled. Her hair was almost completely shock white and her rich honey mahogany skin clearly had distinct jaundice pallor, had it really been that long since he had seen her.

"I have cancer, again," she said, "My liver."

He searched through vague memories, trying to recall when Sylvia previously had cancer. That's right he thought, I think she had a mastectomy. His memories were unclear.

Sylvia's son looked at her with a distant gaze; he smiled and hesitantly touched her cheek.

"It will be okay Sylvia," he said.

He sat beside her for a moment; they exchanged a few words awkwardly.

Fifteen minutes passed. The silent spaces between words grew longer. Fifteen more minutes passed. Sylvia's eldest son was annoyed with himself; he still just couldn't be very comfortable around her. Sylvia looked at her son furtively; she never really could hold his gaze.

His eyes are so intense she always said.

She always wondered if he had found some happiness in life, he always seemed a bit austere and aloof.

Sylvia's son was more of an artist at heart; his muscular lean physique disguised his very esoteric nature. Sylvia understood more about her eldest son then he realized. She followed his life through newspaper clippings. He had won state and national awards for debate and dramatic arts; he had even been chosen as an "Outstanding Teenager of America", there were some sports awards too, she continued with her solitary mental conversation. There were also occasional phone calls and infrequent visits. Their thoughts echoed in the silence between them.

Abruptly he announced that he had to be going.

It's a long drive out of state was his rare but usual exit line.

She always smiled and said she understood, though she knew it wasn't really that far, just a couple of hours or so. Although she remembered that he really disliked driving. Umm, hum; that's right she recalled sorting through mental images of news clippings. It was June or July 1986 when he survived getting hit broadside by that drunk driver.

"How is your neck feeling; legs all right," she asked?

Her son looked at her perplexed. "The accident," she continued.

"OK, most of the time," he answered stiffly.

Sylvia's son promised her that he would come back and see her very soon.

"Umm, hum" she sighed.

This was the first time that he had ever promised a visit and he was definitely a man of his word. She always told her other children how fine of a person she thought he was; Andrea was the only child at home. The others has made it to adulthood and gone about their lives. How she was sorry that they hardly knew their eldest brother. Andrea adored her eldest brother. The anguish in her heart was more than the pain in her gut.

Andrea's giggles and laughter resounded through the house again.

"Bye Sylvia," he called out as the door closed behind him.

Sylvia prayed for a little more time.

Again; the Telephone Rings

Sylvia's son took the rural route from Massachusetts to Rhode Island; The New England fall landscape always fueled his contemplations. He skipped his usual stop at Peaceful Meadows Farm in Bridgewater for homemade ice cream. Flashes of unpleasant childhood school vacations and summers clouded his mind, his heart raced; angrily he told himself *'get over it'*. He arrived home with still a distant look on his face. He opened the door to his town house preoccupied in his thoughts; his children came dashing down the stairs, two sons and a daughter shouted, pape', pape', pape' and rapidly tried to recount their days events. He took a moment to coddle and nudge each of them. His wife was working on the computer. Lastly, his baby girl came toddling over. She had her grandmother's eyes, wide, deep, dark and beautiful with an oriental slant. He gathered her in his arms and peppered her face with affectionate kisses; he looked at his wife somberly. Later on he would go upstairs to check on his infant son who was sleeping.

"My mother is dying," he said, and walked off to the balcony with his baby in arms and other children trailing behind him.

That night he lied awake.

A week later a phone call came pronouncing that his mother was in the hospital.

Sylvia's son took the return route past Peaceful Meadows Farm deep in thought. Barely keeping up to the rural speed limit of forty-five miles per hour, he arrived at the hospital several hours later. He bypassed the lobby elevators and took the stairs up to her room. Sylvia's son looked silently at her in the hospital bed. She seemed so small he thought. He stared at her for several more minutes. He glanced at the clock on the wall; it was almost two o'clock in the afternoon. Hesitantly he sat down beside her. Her eyes fluttered but did not open. Sylvia's breath was very shallow. He looked at Sylvia for more than an hour; finally, he cautiously reached out and took her hand.

He could not remember ever having done that. He touched her cheek with a little hesitation. *He had only done that once before.*

His mother opened her eyes. They were glazed over, obviously from the morphine drip piercing the hand he held within his own. The hours passed, very few words were exchanged in the afternoon stillness. Sylvia closed her eyes again, her breathing a little shallower. He called his father from the bedside telephone to let him know of Sylvia's condition. He was their only child. Born in the youth of their lives, each of them had moved on many years ago.

Sunset came and Sylvia's son left her bedside to make his prayer in the corner of her room. Sylvia awoke to the sound of the chanting of his prayers in Arabic. Her son could feel her awakening presence. After the prayer he sat by her side again, and took her hand, but she had faded off to sleep, breathing even shallower. Hours passed before she woke again, he glanced at the clock; it was nearly 9:30pm.

"It's getting dark," he said.

"You better get going," faintly whispered Sylvia, forcing a smile on her face.

Again, he promised to be back in a few days as he

placed her hand gently by her side. Her son was definitely a man of his promise. Sylvia watched her son's shadowy image fade from the room. She couldn't recall them ever spending that much time together.

Sylvia prayed for a little more time.

A Visitor

Sunday came and went, *Sylvia prayed for a little more time.* Monday passed, and *she prayed for a little more time.*

Tuesday, Sylvia opened her eyes to a handsome visitor with wavy silver hair brushed back from a broad distinguished forehead. He had a thick dark moustache and well shaped graying beard. This cued her that it wasn't her eldest son. It was his father. The years had been very good to her first love, she thought. They reminisced a little and talked about their son; and where their lives had taken them. Together they shared thoughts of death and repeated, together the shahada *(declaration of Islamic Faith)*; 'There is no deity except ALLAH, and Muhammad is his messenger.' Sylvia was very weak now and sleep was constantly heavy upon her.

Sylvia prayed for a little more time as she drifted out of consciousness.

Peaceful Meadows

It was Wednesday; Sylvia's son gathered his family in the car and took the now familiar road to Goddard Hospital in Stoughton, Massachusetts. They passed Peaceful Meadows; the children were excited at the site of the Guernsey's grazing in the field. Sylvia's son didn't stop.

Sylvia eventually opened her eyes to find her son and his family in the room. At first she thought it was a dream. No, it was real. One by one she called her grandchildren by name to her bedside; Jabreel, fourteen years-old, Saraan, twelve years-old; Mekaa'el three years-old, the last time she had see him he was an infant not yet weaned.

"They all look so much like their grandfather," she said. "This little guy could be his twin," she remarked in a failing voice. "Humph," she wheezed.

Her son was amazed that she recognized them and remembered their names. She took their hands and she smiled weakly as she told them how happy she was to see them. The truth was they hardly knew her, but only the present is relevant to the innocent and the dying.

Finally, Sylvia's son took his turn and sat by her side, he placed her youngest granddaughter gently beside her chest. A soft smile crossed her face.

"This is Imanah Mariamme'," he said.

"She looks just like you," faintly whispered his mother, as she caressed the baby's soft loose curly brown her. "Yours was so much longer and jet black," she recalled "I used to keep it braided like a little papoose," she continued to smile ever so weakly. Sylvia's eyes welled with tears. She had held him just like that so long ago.

She couldn't remember holding him since.

Her son could not remember that.

He noticed Sylvia wince in pain; he lifted the baby from her side to his lap. Sylvia had not noticed Abdul-Nuri, her infant grandson.

He sat silent for a moment.

Seizing control over the quaking in his heart, he edged closer to his mother's side and took her hand; slowly he moved his face very close to hers. Their cheeks brushed. In an almost inaudible voice he said,

"Ma, its' all right, I love you." He kissed her cheek with trembling lips.

He could not remember ever doing that.

Sylvia again drifted out of consciousness; *she didn't pray for a little more time.*

Her son and his family slipped from the room and returned home after a stop at Peaceful Meadows Farm.

That night he lied awake, at 2am the telephone rang.

Sylvia died as a result of metastasizing breast cancer. It was in the spring of 1991, she was fifty-four years of age. Today, eleven years later while writing this story; I cried for the first time over my mother's death.

from the records, Ali-Salaam

Do not seek death. Death will find you.
But seek the road which makes death a fulfillment.

Dag Hammarskjöld

The Al Andalus Breast Cancer Trust

In 1991 after enduring two separate mastecomies, my mother died from liver cancer at the age of fifty-four. Her phycians were certain that the liver cancer was directly related to the previous incidences of breast cancer. Now, in 2002 through medical research we know the certainty of this link.

Just before leaving for Africa on a humanitarian mission this past spring I learned that for the second time my sister was diagnosed with cancer after surviving breast cancer several years ago.

One week after returning from Africa my wife was diagnosed with breast cancer. By the Grace of the Almighty and access to excellent medical coverage and care they are both survivors in recovery; for this I am eternally grateful.

Breast Cancer among American women has reached epidemic proportions. It is the second leading cancer among women with more than 200,000 new cases diagnosed annually. Early detection significantly reduces the life threatening risk of breast cancer. Woman detected in the earliest stage currently benefit from an almost 100% survival rate.

Sadly, woman without medical coverage, the poor and minority woman have the highest fatality rate. This is most often due to failure to have the preventative care of an annual mammogram or biannual mammograms for those women at higher risk. The cost of a mammogram ranges from $60 to $150, it varies greatly from community to community and between being performed in a doctor's office or at a hospital. I have established the

Al Andalus Breast Cancer Trust

expressly for the purpose of subsidizing the cost of preventative care for women without any medical coverage. A portion of the proceeds from every copy of this book goes directly to this fund. Give a gift to a friend and a fellow human being. Thank you for your support.

$5 of every copy ordered through
www.becominghuman.net
www.ali-salaam.com
goes directly to this cause.

"Be inspired and share a gift to save a life."
~ *Ali-Salaam*

O mankind! We created you from a single (pair) of a male and a female, and made you into nations and tribes, that ye may know each other (not that ye may despise (each other). Verily the most honored of you in the sight of Allah is (he who is) the most righteous of you. And Allah has full knowledge and is well acquainted (with all things). *The Qur'an 49:13*

Never have I witnessed such sincere hospitality and the overwhelming spirit of true brotherhood as is practiced by people of all colors and races here [Mecca].... this pilgrimage... has forced me to rearrange much of my thought patterns... and toss aside some of my previous conclusions.... In the words and in the actions and in the deeds of 'white' Muslims I felt the same sincerity that I felt among the black African Muslims of Nigeria, Sudan, and Ghana
El Hajj Abdul Malik El Shabazz
(Malcomn X)

Becoming

Becoming human is beyond stature, complexion or intellect.

Becoming human is to celebrate culture, ours and theirs; yours and mine.

Being human is not to champion diversity; but rather to embrace the infinite kaleidoscope and variations of creation; and nurture the uniqueness of each flower in the garden of humanity.

Becoming human ensues from the expressed passions of two momentarily entwined as one.

Being human is to pass through the embryonic oceans within the womb to be born into light, hope and fear admist the cries of a mothers' anguished pain.

Becoming human is to know the warmth of relationship that gives birth to family, tribes and nations;

Being human is understanding the wisdom of religion and tradition and not to be imprisoned by them.

Becoming human is not to worship icons of separation and madness; 'ism's that desensitize us to the humanity of one another. Fascism, religious fanaticism, nationalism, patriotism, racism have led us all to do that.

Becoming human is to feel the despair of the downtrodden, the hopelessness of the refugee, the anguish of the starving, the heartache of the indentured, the futility of the indebted and the anger and apathy of the disenfranchised.

Being human is to face these challenges of life with hope and promise.

Becoming human is to be free from the bonds of the politic elite and live by one's heart and conscience.

Being human is to enjoy the freedom of choosing good over evil and to be steadfast in the mutual enjoining of truth.

Becoming human is learning that ethics are not conditional to the circumstance.

Being human is to respond to the calamities of civilization ethically.

Becoming human is to act in the interest of others without sacrifice but rather with a consciousness to share and give.

Being human is to know that good acts are love, and giving love is equal to being loved.

Becoming human is understanding that the strong are to help all that are weak.

Being human is to act with the consciousness of the heart.

from the records, Ali-Salaam

They said: "In Allah do we put out trust. Our Lord! Make us not a trial for those who practice oppression..." *The Qur'an 10:85*

Trapped In Iraq

There are connections, bonds of relationship that are powerful and common to the human experience. One bond surpasses all others. The relationship of a mother to her children. This is a story of young woman seemingly living an ordinary life in the United States. This was not always so. This is her story.

The horrific tantrum of war can never be realized until it explodes in your ears and brings pangs of anguish to your heart. The desert heat was augmented by the pungent aroma of bombs bursting in air, truly not a patriotic site. The crackling fires of homes and distant wailing just blocks away, deepened the despair of a young American Muslim woman of Iraqi descent.

Baghdad, an ancient renaissance center and modern cosmopolitan city of the Middle East was already falling into ruin. An affluent glorious heritage succumbing to the ambitions of one man destined to be an infamous icon of despotism and megalomania of our age.

Friends and neighbors gathered under pungent smoked filled desert skies for chai and subdued conversation. They would share fears and worries on how close the last shower of terror from the skies came. They talked of their grief for those they knew who were now lost in the mayhem of human desires.

The resounding explosions of missiles and bombs were a malevolent percussion orchestration underscoring Sarah Iman's anguish and desperation. The young American mother's anxiety caused her heart to pound in her chest as heavy as the bombs pounding the homes of Baghdad.

Morning and evening attacks were a ritual; but not one to which she could adjust. At night she would lie catatonic - awake anticipating the evening attack. The windows were left open to avoid shattering as the missiles struck somewhere in the city; each breath of the choking dusty air an omen of an impending catastrophe. Her home still intact, Sarah, felt momentarily relieved by ALLAH's mercy. Sarah's life and that of her young son and daughter for the moment spared a tragic fate; unlike those below who had been obliterated from existence.

After the raid she ran up to the rooftop; she saw the lights of tracer debris from the missiles hailing down upon Baghdad; the cries and wails from the suffering carried on the wind. Fires below roared consuming dwellings and lives, sometimes near; sometimes far. The distraught mother returned down the stairs and peeked in on her children before retiring for a brief fitful sleep.

Sarah weighing barely one hundred pounds at five feet -five inches in height had become physically frail from anxiety over the survival of her four year old son and twenty-one month old daughter. For three days she regurgitated green bile; unable to eat. Sarah's fear for the life of her children was overwhelming; and if she died who would care for her babies? Who would rescue them from this living hell? 'Ya Rabbee' (Oh my Lord)! The extreme stress was beginning to destroy her physical well being. The wrenching pangs in her abdomen seemed unbearable; unending. Her own life not only threatened from living in the midst of a war zone but also from severe dehydration and acute anxiety.

After another three days of continued vomiting and being unable to eat she was faint and exhausted. Sarah was carried to the family car and rushed to the hospital. She entered the door of the hospital to find wounded soldiers and civilians lying upon gurneys and strewn across every square inch of the foyer floor. Medical personnel in crisp white uniforms some stained in blood, dashed about treating the severely traumatized. It was as if the picture story of "Gone With The Wind" had become her bizarre reality. The screaming and wails of the victim's of human madness echoed throughout the hospital.

Placed on a nearby gurney just vacated, she drifted in and out of consciousness; the pandemonium of the event seemed surreal and beyond reason. The moans and wails of victims were a haunting Greek chorus to the tragedy that had become Sarah's life. Sarah gasped and clutched at her abdomen from the wrenching pain. A solitary beat of a bass drum rhythmically resounded in her mind as she drifted out of consciousness again. She awoke briefly as a medical aide injected her with a medicine to relieve the pain and vomiting. They released her to return home.

Twenty four hours later after returning home Sarah displayed a severe allergic reaction to the medicine. The non stop vomiting was replaced by severe itching over her entire body. She scratched and scratched until her skin thin from dehydration and undernourishment tore and began to bleed. After several days of epidermal torture Sarah visited one doctor after another seeking relief. Finally, she found a physician with the competency to diagnose the problem. He gave her an oral medication which in several hours alleviated the itching.

Mornings remained as before. The air raid siren blared heralding another attack. Kettle drums exploded in Sarah's heart in mind. She could never grow accustom to the accelerated panic and fear that plagued each day and that haunted her sleep. As the sirens wailed she would run frantically through the house to find the children. Clinging to them desperately they huddled in the nearest doorway until the latest raid was over. The children it seemed were oblivious to the ever threatening annihilation of their lives; but as a mother the angst of their predicament was well worn on her pretty face. Sarah's complexion had become sallow with deep circles under her eyes. Her reality a nightmare that was readily apparent on her now gaunt delicate countenance.

    The ear-splitting explosions echoed in her mind, asynchronous hollow beats of conga drums that agitated Sarah's thoughts and at times caused her to shudder in fear. She had to get out of Iraq; the lives of her children depended on it. This was a matter of life, sanity or death. Travel abroad was now prohibited and her former employment at the local United Nations office was of no avail to her plight. In the dark restless hours of the night she prayed to ALLAH for a way out; knowing that the only way was to face one of her greatest fears.

    A woman friend shared Sarah's sorrows; she too longed to leave and go to France where she had lived a brief time. Each day after the morning air raids Sarah would share the only comfort to be found conversing with her friend Isra'a. On these visits she and her friend shared their dreams over cups of English tea. They dreamed, prayed and hoped to awake one morning to heavens that did not roar with death and destruction. This was Sarah's greatest desire for her children. She longed to silence the macabre syncopated symphony playing in her mind.

Sarah and Isra'a would talk endlessly of life beyond the calamity and tragedy that exploded daily on the banks of the Tigris River. Each quaking shock surely deepening the burial and grandeur of King Nebuchadnezzar and the splendor of the Abbasid Caliph Mansur; each explosion was one step closer to the demise of her children's future and her own.

"We can not die here, I must find a way, I must," Ya ALLAH, "I must."

Late one morning over tea Isra'a revealed a startling secret to her American companion. She had the telephone number of the President's son-in-law, a government official. Boom, boom quaked the base drum in her heart. Hope, alarm, anticipation flooded Sarah's being. Could this be the answer to her prayer?

More than once she had been rudely treated at the passport office and had lost count of the number of curtly disrupted telephone conversations and the abrupt dismissals by various government persons in previous attempts to return home to America.

Ministry officials would tell her, "Give-up sister and just endure; accept your fate." Now, another faint glimmer of hope; could it be? ALLAHu Alim (GOD only knows)!

On that midsummer morning, the momentarily crisp clear desert skies were backdrop to a dreamy escape of friendship. Now, Sarah's thoughts drifted back to the reality of thundering skies sure to return, in her minds eye she saw the view from the rooftop; blazing fires in the neighborhoods of Baghdad. The tortured screams of victims filling the air and the macabre scene on her emergency visit to the hospital increased the anguish in her heart and mind.

She knew staying in Iraq was no longer an option. 'If there is a will there is away', an American cliché pierced the landscape of her thoughts. My mother used to say that, how good it would be to see her face, she thought. Boom, boom drummed her heart. She would have to take her children and flee this place, where once again mankind had forgotten ALLAH. A place that now only knew synchronized intervals of death and destruction. Yes, she must face her fears.

The distraught American mother recalled in her mind Sura Ar Rad (The Thunder) the words of ALLAH (GOD) revealed by Prophet Muhammad (peace be upon him).

"For each (such person) there are (angels) in succession, before and behind him: They guard him by command of Allah. Verily never will Allah change the condition of a people until they change what is in themselves..."   The Holy Qur'an 13:11

Sarah knew that she would have to face him.

Two friends in suspended time sat breathless on the edge of Isra'a's bed. Do it now their hearts shouted simultaneously in silence. They exchanged a knowing look. The suspended moment passed, Isra'a placed the telephone before Sarah, with anticipation she dialed the number. The administrative aide on the other end of the line promised Sarah a return call from the son-in-law of the President. As she placed the receiver down her friend urged her to return home quickly. Sarah gathered the children in a rush and pushed the stroller between a walk and a run. Her toddler son clung to her hand, feet skimming the baked pavement.

Arriving home she rushed to her room and sat by the phone anxious with anticipation. Sarah wondered if he would really call, would this really be the first step in returning home to America. The ring of the phone jarred Sarah from the angst of her emotions to the reality of the moment. After a brief conversation it was agreed that she would meet him in a public place.

Several hours later Sarah peered into the smoke glass of the Mercedes with bated breath, her frail body quaking, Sarah opened the door to the black bullet proof limousine with trembling hands and got in. Her heart momentarily stopped at the solitary sound of the automatic locks engaging. The middle-aged man with a thick black moustache stared at her with a placid expression. He interrogated her for twenty minutes repeatedly asking her why she wanted to leave Iraq. Sarah was cautious in repeating her answers over and over. "My mother is not well and she would like to see her grandchildren," she stated. She did not vary from this theme. She did her best not to seem to anxious. Finally, it was agreed that she would come to the government ministries in two weeks on Saturday at precisely ten in the morning. She was to follow the directions of the guards precisely.

Fourteen days passed within the surrealism of fourteen years, but finally Sarah watched the rising of Saturday's Sun after completing morning prayers. After carefully inspecting her wardrobe, she selected a white pant suit with appropriate accessories. She arrived at the ministry gates precisely at ten.

The gate guard inspected her with more than an eye for security and then turned his attention to find her name on a list. Sarah, usually quick with a retort to such uncouth behavior, kept quiet. She did not wish to risk jeopardizing this opportunity and there were bigger worries on her mind. After a second visual inspection that seemed more for his personal satisfaction he pointed the way to the ministerial foyer. There she joined a menagerie of human desperation and hopes; people who tempted fate and would entrust their desire to one man.

The presence of the armed guards was lost on Sarah; the apprehension augmented by the twisting knot in her stomach increased by the moment. For an instant she held the gaze of an elderly woman dressed in a black abayah *(traditional covering from head to ankle, revealing only the face and hands)* and wondered why she was there. People looked at one another in silence; the anxious looks of their eyes screamed out in desperation and reverberated in the grand arches of the ministerial chambers. One gentleman sat head bowed ringing his hat. Another woman nervously tapped her feet in a measured cadence. No one dared to converse, perhaps one of them present was a spy for the government.

At intervals of indeterminable length a guard and an administrative aide would enter the foyer and call six names. A small band of desperate hopes would parade behind them and disappear down another corridor. The heel strikes of the small randomly selected ensemble a staccato repercussion augmented by the drumbeat of her heart.

"Sarah, Sarah Iman;" a voice slashed her thoughts and her heel strikes became rhythm to a stranger's percussion symphony.

Sarah, found herself in the company of four other woman and one man. They were ushered to one waiting room after the other. They would sit and wait. Then move through a labyrinth of corridors and chambers, to again sit and wait. The waiting was intimidating and seemed endless.

Sarah's thoughts fleeted between visions of her children at home, her parents in America and the face of the one man who could turn her hopes into her demise in a single word. The waiting continued, again a voice shattered her thoughts, Sarah, Sarah Iman. She stood up quickly, another guard with an automatic rifle as an appendage and another administrative aide's inquisitive examination.

"Yah ukhti, ma taqdareen tashufeen el raes."

"Excuse me, sister you will not be able to see the President." He pointed to her slacks.

The hollow thud of a timpani drum exploded in her heart. Her mind whirling seeking words to plead her case. Desperation and panic flooded her entire being. She found herself in a smothering void, colorless and empty. A voice from far away pierced the fog of confusion that had become her mind.

"Nasawee mauid wara isbu'ain."

"We can make an appointment for you to come back in two weeks," the aide said.

The words drifted on Sarah's consciousness and finally a soft sigh of relief issued from her lips.

Another fourteen days passed within the surrealism of fourteen years, but finally Sarah watched the rising of Saturday's Sun after completing morning prayers. Today, her wardrobe selection was already draped over the closet door. A white long sleeved blouse and white ankle length skirt; with appropriate accessories.

Sarah repeated her routine as before to ensure a precise arrival at the Governmental Ministries. She waited patiently as the ogling guard at the gate went through his routine. In the foyer sat a new collection of aspirations gathered in the hearts of war worn Iraqi people.

"Sarah, Sarah Iman;" again she journeyed with an anonymous group of men and women through the labyrinth of archways, corridors and waiting rooms not recognizing anything from her previous visit.

"Sarah, Sarah Iman," a familiar voice called out. The administrative aide smiled. "The President will see you now." Somewhere a cymbal crashed a missed beat and then a double beat of her heart echoed within her being. Sarah stepped through the doorway and with a furtive gaze saw him sitting behind, a beautifully carved desk. A face she recognized from the wall hangings in every shop in Baghdad.

"As Salaam Aleikum, Mr. President," she hoarsely whispered.

He returned the greeting and beckoned her to sit down. Saddam Hussein sat and with relaxed concentration read the report detailing Sarah's request. The report explained that her parents were in North America; that her mother was ill and that she desired to return for a visit. Sarah was glad she did not have to tell her story; she was unsure if she would be able to hide her emotional desperation. She could not stop the trembling in her hands. He must think I have a palsy she thought.

Sarah could not read his stalwart face. The report concluded stating that she wish to take her children who were both born in Baghdad with her to visit their grandparents. On three occasions he glanced up at her and studied her face. Each instance increased her trepidation; could he sense that she planned to make it more than a visit?

Another suspended moment as she awaited his decision or was it a verdict; would he doom them to a fate of constant "bombs bursting in air". She knew the future of her children's safety rested on the forthcoming pronouncement of President Saddam Hussein.

The President finished reading Sarah Iman's statement and looked up at her; he then reached for a sheet of paper and began to write. Sarah strained her eyes trying to read upside down. Without looking up and in a clear and commanding voice the President stated;

"Man trooheen ela Ameriq salamee ala baba," meaning;

"When you get to America give my salaams to your father."

Looking down at the sea of clouds, Sarah was almost oblivious to the inquiring stares of how she came to be the only woman on the flight to Denmark. Every moment that passed since her meeting with the President was like an eon. She longed to smell the air in Europe. Until now there had been no true relief from her anxiety. By the will of the Almighty in less than a day she would safely arrive in America with her children.

Sarah's gaze returned from the blanket of white

clouds to her precious baby girl sound asleep in her arms. A soft smile came to her lips. Sarah reached and fondly tussled the thick luxurious dark curls of her curious wide-eyed son seated at her side. At last a deep heavy sigh escaped her lips. Not until this moment had her heart stopped racing. It had pounded a staccato rhythm each day as she anxiously awaited her departure from Baghdad.

Now, silent tears fell from her eyes and a heart full of joy and gratitude echoed in silence. ALLAH had answered her prayers.

Sarah Iman's identity has been protected for her safety. She still resides with her family in North America.

from the records, Ali-Salaam

"Let not the wise man glory in his wisdom, let not the mighty man glory in his might, let not the rich man glory in his riches: but let him who gloried glory in this, that he understands and knows me, that I am the Lord who practices steadfast love, justice, and righteousness in the earth; for in these things I delight, " says the Lord.

Jeremiah 9:23-24

I am not an Athenian or a Greek, but a citizen of the world.
     Socrates

"Be inspired and share a gift to save a life."
~ *Ali-Salaam*

Being

Becoming human challenges conformity and challenges us to seek relationships and forge bonds beyond sects, tribes and nations.

Being human means being interdependent not independent.

Becoming human is to know that our common genetic pairings render us to one human family.

Being human is the awareness of our dependence upon the sublime and intangible.

Becoming human is to find no esteem in superiority;

Being human is gratefulness, humility and willingness to accept the miracle that is you and me.

Becoming human is to understand that guilt and innocence are subjective to our experience and that history is subjective to our perspective.

Being human is to bring relief to our common experience.

Becoming human is not the freedom to say and do whatever you want; but rather the freedom to refrain from acts that injure the heart and others.

Being human is freeing the slave, nourishing our young, foregoing ignorance, choosing life.

Becoming human is having the courage to always

seek justice --justice for all.

Being human is being just, and the compassion of the just overrides their own desires.

Becoming human is to voice the silent echoes of the heart; and light the path of justice with words of truth and hope.

from the records, Ali-Salaam

Our lives, if blessed to be led by our heart as well as our minds culminate in a moment of realization and meaning. We fully commit to a life in service. It is at this moment we cease becoming human and start being human.

Ali-Salaam
"On Being Human"
Speech at Seattle Yacht Club

Rebuilding the Lion Mountain

Greg returned from a thirty four day visit to the Republic of Sierra Leone located in West Africa - on the Atlantic Ocean, just above the equator. This trip had a profound impact on his life and brought him new perspective and meaning. This is his story.

Several years ago, I heard the late Texas Congresswoman Barbara Jordan say "One of life's biggest regrets is to see a problem - and have the means to solve it - but fail to take action to do so." In Sierra Leone I witnessed a problem and I knew GOD had given me the means to be part of the solution. I knew that returning to America I would invite others to join with me in helping to solve a problem that may help to save a country.

Last year, Osman Kamara, Sierra Leone's Minister of Trade and Economic Development and Paramount Chief Alimammy Hamidu the First, Chief of the Wara Wara Bofodia Chiefdom of Sierra Leone, visited Seattle and attended World Trade Organization meetings.

Because I had assisted them while they were here in our country they invited me to visit their country. I left for Africa with site seeing and exploring business possibilities in mind. I had never seen Africa; with soccer balls as gifts for children and a speech to deliver to the Freetown Rotary Club I left the chill of the northwest winter for the tropics of the equator.

Little did I know that GOD and man had additional plans for me. What I witnessed and experienced will stay with me for a lifetime and have redefined my life's meaning.

You may not be that familiar with the Lion Mountain - Sierra Leone, so let me describe it. Sierra Leone is tiny by African standards. In fact, it is about the size of North Carolina, and was a longtime British colony until forty years ago.

It's capital is the port city of Freetown.

Freetown sits on a peninsula and forms the third largest natural port in the world. Today, Sierra Leone is a country of more than 4 million people who struggle to exist in this hot, tropical, mosquito-infested climate.

In terms of natural resources, Sierra Leone may be the richest country in the world - it's famous for gold, titanium, iron ore - and especially its diamonds.

Yet, ten years of bloody, mutilating war (now ended) have left the country ravaged, impoverished, and among the poorest on the planet. The brutal civil war between government forces and bands of rebels, motivated by greed for control of diamonds — "blood diamonds," has been one of the most terrifying, inhumane wars in human history and I have witnessed the results.

The Revolutionary United Front (RUF) - a vicious rebel army supported by neighboring Liberia and Libya terrorized the population into submission. Rebel troops kidnapped and enslaved thousands of boys and girls - the males for fighting, the females for sex. They were fed alcohol and drugs, including crack cocaine, and as part of a mystic initiation ritual - forced to drink the blood of victims and sometimes cannibalize them. Facing death themselves, if they refused to cooperate, they wielded machetes and hacked off the arms, legs and feet of nearly twenty thousand people: men, women, children, and even infants.

A horrifying testimony to their torture and man's inhumanity to man is the Morytown Amputee Camp in Freetown. The suffering residents of the camp lived in conditions that are worse than the squalor we permit pigs to live in. More than two thousand men, women and child amputees, who by divine mercy and grace have survived, live in these atrocious conditions. Many of these amputees are forced to beg daily for food on the streets of Freetown because the UN and the Sierra Leone government do not provide rice to the camp.

I left the camp each day praying for a miracle of loaves and fishes to feed the multitudes. For less than seventeen dollars per one hundred pound bag (that's a 50 kilo bag), I could provide enough rice to feed a family of four for two months.

Yet strangely, amidst the squalor and filth of the amputee camp, I found reason to believe and to be hopeful. In the center of the camp was a church that the amputees had named: "Believe the Gospel."

I was moved to take action. I asked the man who had been assigned as my driver to go to the nearest rice warehouse and buy as many one hundred pound bags of rice as we had money for. I have never gone without food before - that's rather obvious - but never have I seen people so hungry, desperately reaching for the rice while mothers held up their babies to be fed.

I attended service at Believe the Gospel Church. It was an open-air shelter with a stack of boxes for an altar. I attended the church service with the amputees and I have never felt such an outpouring of love, nor listened so closely to the message of forgiveness - a message that gave me a new understanding of what it really means to forgive those who trespass

The camp residents invited me to attend a soccer match in the camp. Playing on a rough dirt field, they hobbled on one leg and one crutch with skill and aggressiveness that would tire out and intimidate "normal" teams. Each team player had lost a leg, but none had lost his spirit nor his will to live and play.

I met a very special young amputee; a smiling,

seven year old war orphan boy named "Abu Bakr." When Abu Bakr was five years old the rebels killed his parents and chopped off his right leg below the knee. They left him in the bush to bleed to death. Only GOD could have stopped the bleeding and led rescue workers to him.

I found Abu Bakr in the Morytown Amputee Camp and he stole my heart. My goal right now is to adopt Abu Bakr, to raise him in America and give him access to education and opportunity.

Another surprise awaited me in Sierra Leone. The country itself - besides having an official government - is divided into local chiefdoms. Paramount Chief Alimammy Hamidu the First invited me to his home in the Wara Wara Bofodea Chiefdom.

I left Freetown and headed north in a four wheel drive vehicle. The final thirty-eight miles over incredibly rough roads took three hours and it was worth every minute of it. Because, when I finally arrived in northern Sierra Leone I was presented with the traditional white robe worn only by chiefs and I was proclaimed and inaugurated as an honorary Paramount Chief Alimammy Hamidu the Second.

I learned quickly that honor comes through service and in service responsibility and commitment are paramount. I know that I am returning soon to Sierra Leone because I have to rebuild a bridge that the rebels completely destroyed. The Kamabonkane Bridge allows the farmers of Bofodea to take their crops to market. Engineers and materials exist to fix the bridge - but there's no money.

I am returning to Sierra Leone because the people face a food crisis - a man-made famine that can be prevented. During the war, people fled their village homes to escape rebel attacks. Many settled in Freetown, as the rebels burned and bombed villages, destroyed schools, churches and mosques, confiscated livestock, and burned rice seed supplies, farming and fishing tools.

It will take a long time for Sierra Leone to be able to feed itself again. Now that a peace treaty has been signed, the UN and the Sierra Leone government are telling the people that it is time to leave Freetown and return to their villages. That's good news - except that they are being sent back home with no rice seed to plant, no farm tools and fishing nets to use, or livestock to raise.

Today there is no seed to plant and tomorrow there will be no rice to eat - unless help is given. The twenty-five thousand people of Bofodea are blessed with several fish-filled rivers. Yet they have no nets, fishing gear or boats. I am trying, right now, to raise the funds necessary to buy to those necessities which will enable fishermen to fish and feed their families and take the extra to market.

I am returning to Sierra Leone because I know that the situation is serious and becoming desperate. You may be wondering: "Why should WE care?" People who cannot fill their plates cannot embrace democracy and fill the ballot box. A hungry person becomes an angry person who can pick up a gun when it is not possible to pick up a plow.

I learned a valuable life lesson from my month in West Africa. I recognized that governments do not solve problems. People do. Too often governments are the problem. I believe now, more firmly than ever, that individuals, private businesses and nongovernment organizations, service clubs like Rotary Club International; of which I am a member can accomplish more than most government programs. The United Nations Secretary General agrees with me.

"...more and more business leaders are realizing that they do not have to wait for governments to do the right thing, and indeed they cannot afford to. In many cases, governments only find the courage and the resources to do the right thing when business takes the lead."   *UN Secretary General Kofi Annan*

Several months ago, Sierra Leone's government cancelled its "state of national emergency," because of the desperate needs of the people of Sierra Leone, and the fact that Sierra Leone is cash strapped, has no international credit and is entirely dependent upon the international community for help, I feel an urgency to respond. I am committed to building homes, feeding the hungry, educating children and establishing an adoption program between the United States and Sierra Leone.

There is another reason why I must return to Sierra Leone. A very personal reason. I left my service club Rotary pin in Sierra Leone. I pinned it to Abu Bakr's shirt to assure him that I would return and to remind me of what I was committed to. I intend to bring him to America. It is my hope and desire to raise him in the spirit of life and service; service to mankind that brought us together in the Morytown Amputee Camp.

You know, there's a proverb in Sierra Leone that states: One finger can't pick up a stone. — That's true. But when people put our fingers and hands, resources together, and join our hearts in a common cause, we can move mountains.

On May 21, 2002 a human being named Greg Gourley boarded a flight to Sierra Loan with money, supplies and gifts. He departed to retrieve his service club pin accompanied by this author. By the grace and mercy of the Sublime Immortal Divinity we will assist in rebuilding the Lion Mountain.

from the records, Greg Gourely & Ali-Salaam

"Ali-Salaam was willing to sacrifice himself to come to the aid our people; but more than this he took interest in our families and our future by daring the youth of our grief stricken country to hope and dream and to act."

MACLEOD MANSURAY, FREETOWN, SIERRA LEONE

Ali-Salaam is available for keynote presentations, booksignings, seminars and workshops.

Learn more by visiting
www.ali-salaam.com

$5 of every copy ordered through
www.becominghuman.net
goes directly to aid people in need.

Discover your potential; Enroll in the Dynamic and Exciting Workshop

Leadership for the New Millenium

Becoming Human; Being Human Seminar Series

"What then is the American, this new man?...He is an American, who, leaving behind him all his ancient prejudices and manners, receives new ones from the new mode of life he has embraced, the new government he obeys, and the new rank he holds. He becomes an American by being received in the broad lap of our great Alma Mater. Here individuals of all nations are melted into a new race of men, whose labors and posterity will one day cause great changes in the world."
Michel Guillaume Jean de Crevecoeur
(from Letters from an American Farmer)

A 9-11 Hero

The Hero

A young man certified as an emergency medical technician left his home in the secluded upper east side of Manhattan and boarded the number seven train from Queens to lower Manhattan. Sal, boarded the train at his usual stop; as the train rushed toward his destination, his morning contemplations were shattered by the immense black plumes of smoke billowing in the lower Manhattan skies. He knew that the gravity of the human tragedy must be great.

In addition to being an EMT, Sal was also a police cadet and was applying to medical school. He lived a life demonstrating his courage and compassion. Sal did what any other red blooded *'All American'* young man would do. He disembarked at the stop nearest to the calamity; using his police ID he hitched a ride to the site of the emergency.

The adrenaline already coursed through his body and each second was an eon; he was certain his skills were urgently needed; needed by many. Sal and the other rescue service personnel finally arrived at the World Trade Center Plaza. They quickly exited their vehicle; the gravity of the unfolding events became more apparent every step they took. Sal jogged toward ground zero engulfed in the pandemonium of a war zone.

Flashing his police ID and moving like a football halfback, Sal worked his way through the outer cordons and fleeing people. Soon, he joined streams of other rescue personnel charging forward into the Twin Towers; committed only to saving the lives of others. This is the best possible scenario that police could reconstruct of what happened to Sal that day. *Like many other New Yorkers on that day, he would never return home.*

A Suspect

Law enforcement agencies convened in New York City in the waning days in the summer of 2001. The American people had not experienced such an event since April 19, 1996; the date of the Oklahoma City bombing. Local police, FBI, CIA, FEMA and special task forces compiled lists of possible suspects. One list contained the name Mohammed Hamdani. He was a graduate in chemistry from Queens College. Mohammed also worked at Rockefeller University as a lab analyst and had not reported for work. His family could not account for his disappearance or his failure to respond to his cell phone. Many investigators were certain that this clearly indicated that he was one of the prime suspects connected to the attacks. Several days passed and Hamdani could still not be found lending credence to the opinion of his nefarious involvement in the heinous acts that took place on the morning of September 11th. Mohammed's family was questioned and the suspicion of their relative foreshadowed there foreboding on his whereabouts and feared demise.

Mohammed's parents were certain that they had inculcated the virtuous moral standards of their faith in their son. They taught him that *'he must want for others, what he wants for himself; that taking a single innocent life was as if one had slaughtered all of humanity.'* They were unwavering and confident in telling authorities that he had no connection to the malevolent actions that had struck the hearts and shocked the minds of all the people of their adoptive homeland.

The Hamdani family arrived in the United States in 1979. Mohammed was only a toddler, not even two years of age. He had grown to be an intelligent, studious and caring person. Their son could in no way be linked to this treacherous tragedy. Mr. and Mrs. Hamdani feared that he was a victim of the atrocity and insisted on this to authorities. Suspicion remained and as days passed their only hope was a dubious one. *Perhaps Mohammed was among the dozens of Muslim and Arab men secretly detained and being questioned by law enforcement authorities.*

The Patriot

Sal did not live to reach his twenty-fourth birth anniversary. He had no known reason to be near Ground

Zero; it became apparent that he rushed toward the inferno of the twin towers in a selfless act that cost him his life. Sal, short for Salman was also nicknamed, Young Jedi; he was a Star Wars buff. Like a courageous Jedi Knight he did not flinch in the face of eminent danger; he loved life, people and his country. Thirty days, later while all of America was still reeling from the horror in shock of September 11th, he was honored by our congress.

October 11, 2002 a U.S. Senate bill 1510; The Patriot Act, was passed and mentioned Sal, by name as an example of patriotism under section 102 (6).

"Many Arab-Americans and Muslim Americans have acted heroically during the attacks on the United States, including *Mohammed Salman Hamdani*, a 23 year-old New Yorker of Pakistani descent, who is believed to have gone to the World Trade Centre to offer rescue assistance and is now missing."

A Martyr

It was Wednesday, March 20, 2002; the police arrived at the home of Sal's parents, Saleem and Talat Hamdani. His remains had been identified. Sal, a

Muslim, an American who had been a suspect was indeed a fallen hero; a patriot and a martyr.

On Friday, April 5, 2002 six months later Mohammed Salman Hamdani's mother eulogized her son at his funeral in a masjid *(mosque)* in Manhattan.

She said, "The day you were born I came to know the joy of motherhood. Today I understand its pain. Salman, you wouldn't let me celebrate your graduations. *This is nothing to be proud of, Mama, you said; I will tell you when to celebrate.* So you did. You told the world loud and clear when to celebrate—today."

Talat Hamdani, Salman's mother has established a memorial fund in her son's name at Rockefeller University to provide scholarships to American students of Pakistani descent who wish to pursue medicine.

She states, "My son's actions that day are a glimmer of hope for the community."

His father Saleem, who owns a general store in Brooklyn says, "His example is now a part of United States history."

from the records, Ali-S

"You are never given a wish without being given the power to make it true."

Richard, Bach "Illusions"

"Sooner or later, all the peoples of the world will have to discover a way to live together in peace, and therby transform this pending cosmic elegy into a creative psalm of brotherhood. If this is to be acheived, man must evolve for all human conflict a way which rejects revenge, aggression and retaliation."

Dr. Marth Luther King, Jr.
(Acceptance of Nobel peace Prize, 10th of December 1964)

Become Human

Being human is to see potential, imagine the possibilities and believe in the probability; and to act extraordinarily.

Becoming human is a process guided by self, and nurtured by experience.

Being human imprints fond memories in the hearts of others; and resonates in celestial harmonics.

Becoming human is to view from the mountain top the balance and beauty of the landscape and to see beyond the horizon.

Being human is to help others climb the mountain.

Becoming human is to bask in the warmth of winters sun and drink from the shade on a summer afternoon.

Being human is to light a fire in the hearth of humanity by serving all those in need.

Becoming human is to forgo privilege. Assumption of privilege is the heart of hatred; hatred is the heart of prejudice, and prejudice is the heart of bigotry.

from the records, Ali-Salaam

Former Israeli Minister of Defense Moshe Dayan in 1950 stated:

"Using the moral yardstick mentioned by [Moshe Sharett], I must ask: Are [we justified] in opening fire on the [Palestinian] Arabs who cross [the border] to reap the crops they planted in our territory; they, their women, and their children? Will this stand up to moral scrutiny? We shoot at those from among the 200,000 hungry [Palestinian] Arabs who cross the line [to graze their flocks]—— will this stand up to moral review? Arabs cross to collect the grain that they left in the abandoned [term often used by Israelis to describe the ethnically cleansed] villages and we set mines for them and they go back without an arm or a leg. . . . [It may be that this] cannot pass review, but I know no other method of guarding the borders then tomorrow the State of Israel will have no borders."

(Righteous Victims, p. 275)

Children of the Prophets

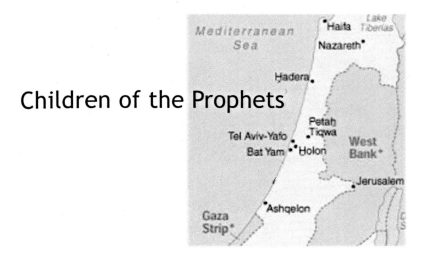

On Hallow Ground

Nadia Ali reminisces on her romantic childhood growing up in the mystique of the land that was *host to the prophets*. The lists read as a "Who's Who" in Judaic, Biblical and Qur'anic scripture. Nuh (Noah), Lut (Lot), Khidr (Melchezadek), Ibrahim (Abraham), Ilyas (Elijah), Hud, Shu'aib (Jethro), Yosha' (Joshua) his tomb near Salt, Musa (Moses) the site of his death on Mount Nebo, Harun (Aaron) his tomb in Petra, Dawud (David) his Shrine in Mazar Al-Shamali near Kerak, Sulayman (Solomon), Ayyub (Job), Yahya (John the Baptist), Isa (Jesus), and prophet Muhammad peace be upon them all lived or journeyed in the ancient lands of Jordan.

Sipping chai and nibbling on an occasional pistachio; Nadia Ali's eyes glimmer with fond memories. She speaks animatedly in Arabic as she recalls her travels as a girl with her beloved father Jiwad. Nadia tells us of the ancient ruins that grace the desert plains and her visit to the Roman Decapolis City of Jerash- one of the best preserved Roman cities. She becomes momentarily quiet as she recounts the austere Crusader Fortress of Kerak.

I am amazed at her recall, as is her son Qassim who graciously interprets to compensate for my limited Arabic vocabulary. I am enraptured as Nadia Ali tells me of the majesty of Petra. A jewel of a city carved out of rock by the ancient Nabateans; a city that dazzles reflecting the colors of the setting desert sun.

She is a picturesque vision of a noble elderly Arab woman who considers herself a Philistine (Palestinian) though she notes her nomadic origins going back to the most famous of ancient lands, Egypt. I am grateful for Nadia and Qassim's visit before they depart from the United States. She is anxious to return home.

Home to Nadia Ali is the country of Jordan. Among the many historical places she speaks of is

Jordan's Valley of Shuaib. The Valley of Shuaib is home to the ancient ruins of Tell Iktanu and Tell Hammam. Tell Iktanu site is located just south of the Wadi Rama/Hisban in the southeast Jordan Valley, about fifteen kilometers east of Jericho on the east side of the Jordan River. Tell Iktanu's ancient people built strategically upon natural rock formations near the foothills.

Three kilometers north is Tell Hammam lying on the south bank of the perennial Wadi Kafrain overlooking the southeast Jordan Valley. A good water supply supports a richer local flora. There are warm springs on the south side of the *tell*; it is hypothesized that these springs fed baths in the late Roman/Byzantine periods.

I can still see the child wonder and amazement in her eyes as Nadia speaks of the rich legacy of her homeland.

"How I love Jordan," she says "I grew up primarily in the city of Salt; being of nomadic lineage we traveled a lot."

Nadia describes with warmth in her voice an ancient town that was once the capital of Jordan.

"It is only a half-hour drive northwest from it's modern day capitol, Amman;" she tells me.

In my minds eye I am transported back in time to a town of picturesque streets and spectacular houses dating back to Ottoman rule in the fifteenth century of the Common Era. The architecture is outstanding with it's defining long-arched windows. Traditional skills of ceramics, weaving, silkscreen printing, and dyeing are still admired and practiced today.

"This was my world without borders," she states. "From Salt to what is Yaffo; modern day Tel Aviv."

1948

My guest, a gentile matriarch grows quiet for a moment. Her dark eyes grow deep and she speaks to Qassim in a hushed tone. She looks at me again.

"She wants to tell you something important," Qassim tells me; "But you must promise her that you will change the names of all the people in this story who are still living including mine."

I looked at him quizzically.

"My mother insists," he says, "The memories and the wounds grow deep."

I agree.

In 1948 Nadia Ali was thirteen years of age. In

1948 Nadia's world without borders would end. Her face tightens and her sorrow is readily apparent.

Nadia looks at me in eerie silence.

Her voice quivers slightly as she says, "I remember the massacres."

Nadia Ali tells me a story all too familiar even today. A village would be surrounded by Israeli soldiers and they would kill almost everyone. They would steal the infants and take them back to Israel and give them to Israeli families. A few might escape she explained and would flee to the next village to warn the people there.

"One such place was known to us as Deer Yasin," she notes. A shadow comes across her face as she grimaces, "There my cousin Yunnus, a noted scholar and teacher was murdered."

This time the soldiers left one point of escape towards the newly defined Jordan. This was their strategy she sorrowfully explained; devastate the people in one place in order to terrorize the other nearby towns and villages into fleeing to Jordan.

We have historically been a nomadic people Bedouins, Coptics, Chechnyians, Egyptians, Arabs, Jews, Christians and Muslims all sharing this historically rich wonderful place. Tragically in 1948 her precious world had become a brutal and horrific place.

"We have not known any peace since then," states Nadia.

"This was very confusing and appalling;" she tells me, "My entire childhood I had lived with Christians and Jews. We were friends and neighbors happily living together. There had been minor conflicts but nothing like this."

Nadia tells of families so diverse in ethnicity sharing one culture, each still upholding the traditions and religion of their forefathers. I learn how they often picnicked together and traveled to many of the wonderful places together throughout the Holy Land from Salt to Yaffo (modern day Tel Aviv).

As Nadia Ali became a young woman, life in this wondrous and beautiful place was shattered.

Nadia Ali pauses again in silence as a somber pallor shadows her face.

"We had a very dear neighbor and family friend. Salim Al Yahud; Salim the Jew; this is what we called him," she informs me in a subdued voice.

"In those days," she states "people were usually identified by their tribe."

Salim, his Polish wife and two daughters shared religious celebrations with the Ali family. Nadia muses as she speaks to me of Salim's wife.

"I often worried for her," she notes. "She did not speak Hebrew or Arabic."

As the dearest of friends Nadia recounts how they shared many site seeing excursions and picnics.

Again, Nadia is silent.

She tells me of the tragedy of the borders sealing down and Salim being in Israel and his daughters trapped in Jordan.

"Our community would not stand for that;" she continues, "Everyone banded together and devised a plan to reunite Salim with his family. There was no thought of them being Jews and us Muslims. My father, *(May ALLAH accept his deed)* decided to smuggle Salim's daughters to him."

It was necessary for them to wait for a time of relative calm and for the borders to be relaxed for general travel. In that time the public works infrastructure was not nearly as developed as the present. What is presently a four hour trip; was then a twelve hour ordeal.

Jiwad's plan was to travel as in the past on

excursions to popular sites. Salim's daughters would dress in the traditional Muslim hijab like Nadia's sisters.

Jiwad, Nadia's father, hired an unmarked taxi for twenty Jordanian Dinars.

"In those days," she remarks, "That would purchase twenty acres of land."

Nadia wants me to understand the sacrifice that her Muslim family was willing to make for their beloved Jewish friends. The sojourn began with much anticipation, trepidation and prayers. Fortunately, passports and visas had not become a custom. She tells me again of departing Salt after Fajr *(dawn prayers)* and passing through the Valley of Shuaib, then to No Shorna to Sharia'a.

"These places have been erased from existence and their names erased from history," she sighs.

They rested briefly from their hot and arduous passage, before continuing their journey on to Jericho. They passed through the many small villages until they finally arrived in Jerusalem. Here they would all eat and pray at Masjid Al Aqsa for Dhur *(noon prayers)* and Asr *(late afternoon prayers)*. After several hours rest in Jerusalem the blended family resumed their course to Yaffo; finally reaching the villages by late evening.

A Reunion

Salim Al Yahud placed his Torah by the side of the lamp to answer the knock at his door. He was not expecting visitors. As Salim approached the door he could hear muffles hushing tones. He opened the door to find his daughter and friends standing before his eyes. Astonished and elated, he greeted them with smiles, embraces and tears. He fondly held Jiwad's hands politely scolding him for taking such risks. Most of all he was thankful for his friend's sacrifice.

The next day still masquerading as an extended family, they celebrated there reunion on the banks of the Mediterranean. Nadia smiles as she recalls the clear blue waters of the ancient sea. They sang, laughed and enjoyed plump dates, fresh baked breads and pastries, curried lamb and many culinary delights. The driver, too, basked in the wonderful weather and the happiness of the occasion. Sunset came, Jiwad led his family in prayer, while his dear companion, Salim and his family sat quietly nearby. Shortly thereafter they returned to the home of Salim for tea and more reminiscing. The next morning they departed for Jordan.

Sadness is reflected in the quiet tears forming in

Nadia's eyes. She never saw her friends again.
More silence.
The weight of the moment settled upon all our hearts; each of us lost in our thoughts.

Hope for Tomorrow

After what seemed an eternal moment, I turned to Qassim and said; "Ask your mother what are her hopes for Palestine and Israel."

She responded simply this; "I have no hatred of Israelis or Jews. We are all the 'Children of Abraham." Nadia momentarily paused and sighed; "When I see the forlorn faces of the children in the streets of Israel and Palestine I long for them to hold hands and dance at the sea.

Again silence.

In a quiet firmness she states, "I want the violence to end; I want us all to be able to share this precious land and to eat together again, in peace."

Nadia Ali escorted by Qassim, returned to the land of the prophets. May ALLAH give her the breath and strength to realize her hope. May we all remember the message of the prophets ~ peace.

from the records, Ali-Salaam

Throughout my entire life the perpetual cycle of violence in Palestine and Israel has been unbroken. Each side has forgotten their humanity and now, it seems that they only seek to excel one another in hatred and transgression. Amongst the leadership and the masses there are far too many Palestinians and Israelis; and not enough human beings, residing in this desert place we call the Holy Lands. ~ *Ali-Salaam* ~

". . . Let us not today fling accusation at the murderers. What causes have we to complain about their fierce hatred to us? For eight years now, they sit in their refugee camps in Gaza, and before their eyes we turn into our homestead the land and villages in which they and their forefathers have lived.

Statement of Israeli Minister of Defense Moshe Dayan in an oration at the funeral of an Israeli farmer killed by a Palestinian Arab in April 1956: (Iron Wall, p. 101)

On the authority of Anas bin Malik, the servant of the messenger of Allah, that the Prophet Muhammad (peace be upon him) said :

"None of you [truely] believes until he wishes for his brother what he wishes for himself."

related by Bukhari and Muslim

For each (such person) there are (angels) in succession, before and behind him: They guard him by command of Allah. Verily never will Allah change the condition of a people until they change what is in themselves. But when (once) Allah willeth a people's punishment, there can be no turning it back, nor will they find, besides Him, any to protect.   *The Qur'an 13:11*

"He that would give up few essential liberties for a little temporary safety, deserves neither the liberty nor the safety."
Benjamin Franklin

A Matter of Conscience

Let it not be said that people in the United States did nothing when their government declared a war without limit and instituted stark new measures of repression. The signers of this statement call on the people of the US to resist the policies and overall political direction that have emerged since September 11 and which pose grave dangers to the people of the world.

We believe that peoples and nations have the right to determine their own destiny, free from military coercion by great powers. We believe that all persons detained or prosecuted by the US government should have the same rights of due process. We believe that questioning, criticism, and dissent must be valued and protected. We understand that such rights and values are always contested and must be fought for.

We believe that people of conscience must take responsibility for what their own governments do - we must first of all oppose the injustice that is done in our own name.

Thus we call on all Americans to resist the war and repression that has been loosed on the world by the Bush administration. It is unjust, immoral and illegitimate. We choose to make common cause with the people of the world.

We too watched with shock the horrific events of September 11. We too mourned the thousands of innocent dead and shook our heads at the terrible scenes of carnage - even as we recalled similar scenes in Baghdad, Panama City and, a generation ago, Vietnam.

We too joined the anguished questioning of millions of Americans who asked why such a thing could happen.

But the mourning had barely begun, when the highest leaders of the land unleashed a spirit of revenge. They put out a simplistic script of "good vs. evil" that was taken up by a pliant and intimidated media. They told us that asking why these terrible events had happened verged on treason. There was to be no debate. There were by definition no valid political or moral questions. The only possible answer was to be war abroad and repression at home.

In our name, the Bush administration, with near unanimity from Congress, not only attacked Afghanistan but arrogated to itself and its allies the right to rain down military force anywhere and anytime. The brutal repercussions have been felt from the Philippines to

Palestine.

The government now openly prepares to wage all-out war on Iraq - a country which has no connection to the horror of September 11. What kind of world will this become if the US government has a blank cheque to drop commandos, assassins, and bombs wherever it wants?

In our name the government has created two classes of people within the US: those to whom the basic rights of the US legal system are at least promised, and those who now seem to have no rights at all.

The government rounded up more than 1,000 immigrants and detained them in secret and indefinitely. Hundreds have been deported and hundreds of others still languish today in prison. For the first time in decades, immigration procedures single out certain nationalities for unequal treatment.

In our name, the government has brought down a pall of repression over society. The president's spokesperson warns people to "watch what they say". Dissident artists, intellectuals, and professors find their views distorted, attacked, and suppressed. The so-called Patriot Act - along with a host of similar measures on the state level - gives police sweeping new powers of search and seizure, supervised, if at all, by secret proceedings before secret courts.

In our name, the executive has steadily usurped the roles and functions of the other branches of government. Military tribunals with lax rules of evidence and no right to appeal to the regular courts are put in place by executive order. Groups are declared "terrorist" at the stroke of a presidential pen. We must take the highest officers of the land seriously when they talk of a war that will last a generation and when they speak of a new domestic order. We are confronting a new openly imperial policy towards the world and a domestic policy that manufactures and manipulates fear to curtail rights.

There is a deadly trajectory to the events of the past months that must be seen for what it is and resisted. Too many times in history, people have waited until it was too late to resist. President Bush has declared: "You're either with us or against us." Here is our answer:

We refuse to allow you to speak for all the American people. We will not give up our right to question. We will not hand over our consciences in return for a hollow promise of safety. We say not in our name. We refuse to be party to these wars and we repudiate any inference that they are being waged in our name or for our welfare. We extend a hand to those around the world suffering from these policies; we will show our solidarity in word and deed.

We who sign this statement call on all Americans to join together to rise to this challenge. We applaud and support the questioning and protest now going on, even as we recognize the need for much, much more to actually stop this juggernaut. We draw inspiration from the Israeli reservists who, at great personal risk, declare "there is a limit" and refuse to serve in the occupation of the West Bank and Gaza.

We draw on the many examples of resistance and conscience from the past of the US: from those who fought slavery with rebellions and the underground railroad, to those who defied the Vietnam war by refusing orders, resisting the draft, and standing in solidarity with resisters. Let us not allow the watching world to despair of our silence and our failure to act. Instead, let the world hear our pledge: we will resist the machinery of war and repression and rally others to do everything possible to stop it.

FROM:
Ali-Salaam, author
Michael Albert
Laurie Anderson
Edward Asner, actor
Russell Banks, writer
Rosalyn Baxandall, historian
Jessica Blank, actor/playwright
Medea Benjamin, Global Exchange
William Blum, author
Theresa Bonpane, executive director, Office of the Americas
Blase Bonpane, director, Office of the Americas
Fr Bob Bossie, SCJ
Leslie Cagan
Henry Chalfant, author/filmmaker
Bell Chevigny, writer
Paul Chevigny, professor of law, NYU
Noam Chomsky
Stephanie Coontz, historian, Evergreen State College
Kia Corthron, playwright
Kevin Danaher, Global Exchange
Ossie Davis
Mos Def
Carol Downer, board of directors, Chico (CA) Feminist Women's Health Center

Originally published titled "Not In Our Name"

Roxanne Dunbar-Ortiz, Professor, California State University
Eve Ensler
Leo Estrada, UCLA professor, Urban Planning
John Gillis, writer, professor of history, Rutgers
Jeremy Matthew Glick, editor of Another World Is Possible
Suheir Hammad, writer
David Harvey, distinguished professor of anthropology, CUNY Graduate Centre
Rakaa Iriscience, hip hop artist
Erik Jensen, actor/playwright
Casey Kasem
Robin DG Kelly
Martin Luther King III, president, Southern Christian Leadership Conference
Barbara Kingsolver
C Clark Kissinger, Refuse & Resist!
Jodie Kliman, psychologist
Yuri Kochiyama, activist
Annisette & Thomas Koppel, singers/composers
Tony Kushner
James Lafferty, executive director, National Lawyers Guild/LA
Ray Laforest, Haiti Support Network
Rabbi Michael Lerner, editor, Tikkun magazine
Barbara Lubin, Middle East Childrens Alliance
Staughton Lynd

Anuradha Mittal, co-director, Institute for Food and Development Policy/Food First
Malaquias Montoya, visual artist
Robert Nichols, writer
Rev E Randall Osburn, executive vice president, Southern Christian Leadership Conference
Grace Paley
Jeremy Pikser, screenwriter
Jerry Quickley, poet
Juan Gumez Quiones, historian, UCLA
Michael Ratner, president, Centre for Constitutional Rights
David Riker, filmmaker
Boots Riley, hip hop artist, The Coup
Edward Said
John J Simon, writer, editor
Starhawk
Michael Steven Smith, National Lawyers Guild/NY
Bob Stein, publisher
Gloria Steinem
Alice Walker
Naomi Wallace, playwright
Rev George Webber, president emeritus, NY Theological Seminary
Leonard Weinglass, attorney
John Edgar Wideman
Saul Williams, spoken word artist
Howard Zinn, historian

The Guardian, Friday June 14, 2002
Reprinted with Permissions

VISIT THIS WEB SITE
http://www.nion.us/

" I believe there are more instances of the abridgment of freedom of the people by gradual and silent encroachments of those in power than by violent and sudden usurptions."
Presidnet James Madison

"The finest emotion of which we are capable is the mystic emotion. Herein lies the germ of all art and all true science. Anyone to whom this feeling is alien, who is no longer capable of wonderment and lives in a state of fear is a dead man. To know that what is impenatrable for us really exists and manifests itself as the highest wisdom and the most radiant beauty, whose gross forms alone are intelligible to our poor faculties - this knowledge, this feeling ... that is the core of the true religious sentiment. In this sense, and in this sense alone, I rank myself among profoundly religious men."
Albert Einstein
"Science, Philosophy, and Religion, A Symposium",

The Universe

The word universe is derived from the Latin words 'uni' and 'veras'; that is to say there is 'one truth'. The truth of the universe is that its' source of origination slowly unfolds Itself to us. Science only confirms that there is a Greatest Intelligence beyond our full understanding.

Our discovery through linear, theoretical postulation ignites a reverence of what is undoubtedly a sentient self perpetuating inexhaustible source. This source yielding before our eyes and perceptions, It's sublime mystery, awesome power, diverse simple and complex forms.

The net of connectivity between quantum particles, matter, energy and biological life is inexplicable. Our inability to communicate a complete unchanging scientific explanation is a reality of our human limitation. Religions, philosophical doctrines and theorems fill the void where our reason and comprehension fail us as created beings.

The dogma of religion at times entraps us in a

milieu of pathetic discourse and at worse violent and despicable acts.

The spiritual enlightenment leads the faithful to embrace the sojourn of our realities as a spiritual evolution of the self. Through understanding our interdependent empathic relationships as part of this glorious existence we can achieve an ethical social order.

The Universal Human Creed

~ We recognize that our capacity for intelligent behavior is necessary and an integral part of the *One-Truth*; this Universe. Individually and thereby collectively we shall endeavor to balance our lives and ambitions.

~ As sentient beings whose actions profoundly effect the physical existence surrounding us, we shall be respectful and compassionate to all life.

~ We know that each and every human deserves a life of dignity and hope. Therefore intelligently we shall strive to establish social order based on sustainable ways of life that are not predicated on privilege; but rather the inalienable right of all to peace and justice.

~ The human existence of body, mind and soul (the intangible) is self-evident to each of us. Our need to express ourselves through our talents and abilities is inherent to the meaning of life.

~ Our need to do this interdependently is paramount. Doing so challenges us to 'heart-thought'; a balance of compassion and reason.

~ The only entitlement for everyone is a life with dignity; that is beyond basic needs. That individual and social communication through language, culture, art and entertainment should never demean or hold contemptuous commentary and or actions upon one another.

~ Our quest to understand life through science, aesthetic and religious feelings is unique to our humanity. Differences in relating to the Universe and each other in this manner are not a legitimate basis for conflict.

~ At all times a dialogue for dignity, embracing core values of being human and measuring of our actions against these values, is an integral step in the realization and actualization of a just society.

from the records, Ali-Salaam

I have not the shadow of a doubt that any man or woman can achieve what I have. If he or she would make the same effort and cultivate the same hope and faith.
Mahatma Gandhi, 1869

Doubt sees the obstacles, Faith sees the way.
Doubt sees the darkest night, Faith sees the day.
Doubt dreads to take a step, Faith soars on high.
Doubt whispers, "Who believes?" Faith answers "I".
Anonymous

Two Prayers

The Bishop

Bishop George Biguzzi is about 5' 5" tall, appropriately balding and graying in a manner that appears to dignify his mien. It is evident by his black suit and white collar he is a member of the clergy. An American of Italian descent born in Milwaukee, Wisconsin and has lived in Africa for over 20 years. An elegant trace of an Italian accent augments his soft pleasing voice.

Bishop Biguzzi leads a parish in Makeni, the second largest city in the West African country of Sierra Leone. In May of this year (2002 C.E.) the people of Sierra Leone had their first election in eleven years. Hope and promise fills the hearts of the indigenous people and those like Bishop Biguzzi who have adopted this homeland through a life in service.

Less than two years ago Sierra Leone was under a hostile siege from rebel forces being backed by political powers outside of Sierra Leone. I stopped briefly in Makeni on my return from a week long journey in the northern provinces of Sierra Leone. Climbing from the back of the Land Rover where I had been wedged in amongst five other passengers, baggage, a half-dozen fifty kilogram bags of rice and a couple of live chickens, I squinted through the mid-afternoon glare at the faded buildings. Shielding my eyes I stiffly pirouetted counterclockwise and gazed upward where the four story buildings of the town square met the sky line. Bullet holes pockmarked the worn cement surfaces.

The visage of Makeni was a constant reminder of the grief and strife that had ended not long ago. One of my indigenous travel companions noted 'almost everyone you see here is a former rebel; this was their center'. I later learned that the vast majority of people fled to the capitol city of Freetown knowing of the rebels impending arrival. Those who remained suffered mortally.

    Bishop Biguzzi integrated himself through service as a pillar of that community. Twice he had served as President of the local Rotary Club in addition to his responsibilities in the church. He is liked and respected by the citizens of Makeni. Quietly and softly he speaks of the night the rebels attacked. The rebels had no opposition.

    There were members of the parish staff who did not survive the night. Three nuns were outside the rectory helping the injured in the streets. They were captured, tortured and killed. One of the priests was shot and left to die in the street.

    The infamous child soldiers wired on crack cocaine or heroin were the first to appear carrying their AK-47s and machetes. The cries and screams of the innocent echoed in the sanctuary heralding the arrival of the child-soldiers. The Bishop was inside the rectory with several nuns and staff when the rebels broke through the door ordering them to go outside. Bishop Biguzzi recognized many of the rebels. Some had been students in the Catholic schools of Makeni; some had attended mass. A few others had been given communion.

    The Bishop knew of the drug induced rage that

the child-soldiers were in. He was all too well aware of the brutality that the first wave of rebel forces inflicted upon the people when they stormed a town or village. He was certain that if he and his staff left the sanctuary of the rectory they would be killed. He was grateful that they had some respect for the church for he was certain that if this was not true, they would all be killed on the spot. As a man of the cloth, he did what years of training and belief had taught him.

First, instinctively and prayerfully he picked up a cross on the table and held it up to the rebels holding the cross between the rebels and his co-workers. His eyes flashed to the wall statue of the Virgin Mary and then he began to pray. He prayed St. Joseph's prayer of protection and the 'Lord's Prayer'.

Bishop Biguzzi prayed not for his life but for the lives of the nuns and staff members standing behind him. He tells of an inner peace that enveloped him as he prayed and a ring of angels that appeared and surrounded him and his staff. He was at peace. Without a word being said, the rebels lowered their guns, turned and left the rectory. Bishop Biguzzi and his staff went out the back door where his car was parked and escaped to Freetown.

"For my Protector is Allah, Who revealed the Book (from time to time), and He will befriend the righteous."
> *The Qur'an 7:196*

The Chief

The north Guinea border has been plagued with attacks on both sides of the border. Armed Forces Revolutionary Council (AFRC) and Revolutionary United Front (RUF), rebel/terrorist forces in the east and the north of Sierra Leone are deliberately and arbitrarily killing and torturing unarmed civilians. A deliberate and systematic campaign of killing, rape and mutilation - called by the rebel forces "Operation no living thing" began in April 1998. Tens of thousands of civilians, traumatized by the vicious attacks, have fled to Conakry (the capital Guinea) or even left for Freetown, Sierra Leone. Guinea is a refuge for nearly a half million refugees from Sierra Leone and Liberia, as is Freetown.

Although the exact number of those killed is unknown, it is likely to be several thousand, many of them women and children. More than two hundred people were killed during an attack on the village of

Yifin, in the Northern Province.

Late one evening while staying in the township of Bofodea, I sat on the porch, star gazing and refreshed myself in the rare cool air, a young boy comes and takes my hands;

"The Chief wishes to speak with you he says."

The boy leads me by the hand to the rear of the house where Chief Alimammy beckons me to sit at a small wooden table leveled by folded paper under two of the legs. He instructs the boy to send for some chai, he immediately dashes through the side door to the outdoor kitchen that I had seen earlier that day.

"I have something I want to tell you," the tall lean elder says. I adjust myself on the hard chair perching my elbows on the table and wait for him to begin.

"I want to tell you what happened to me the night the rebels came." Chief Alimammy's face is set firm, he gestures to a large antique sepia tone photo on the mantel. I can see in a glance that it is him in full military dress splendor but at least twenty or thirty years ago.

"That was during the Congo war," he states. "I was a military man for a long time, but never in the rules of engagement have I witnessed the horror of these punks masquerading as freedom fighters." The muscles in the jaw of his lean face tightened.

I sat focused intently; I am too shy to ask if I can go to my quarters and retrieve a notebook and pen.

The Chief explains that before he came to the *'States'* last year that an assassin squad of twenty-five men had been sent to kill him. I remember his visit for medical treatment. I never new the reasons why, until now.

"I could feel them coming, "ALLAHu Akbar (GOD is truly the Great)," he exclaims. He tells of young men equipped with rifles and machetes stealthily approaching his compound.

"ALLAHu Akbar," he reiterates.

"I thought of my wives, children and our people who had fled; I could not comprehend the aim of the RUF or what they sought to achieve in the end. They have destroyed so much. What spoils will there be for the victor," he explains.

"ALLAHu Akbar, ALLAH, Alhumdulilah," he exclaims again. "I armed myself with a cudgel."

Chief Alimammy Hamidu goes on to tell how he defeats seven of the twenty-five assassins in hand to hand combat. He thinks this feat was a miracle in itself.

"ALLAH gave me the strength," he states.

The Chief further explains that after disabling the seventh rebel he was physically spent. He had sustained a wound to the head from a bayonet and was bleeding profusely.

"I looked at the faces of the remaining boys in the dark; I faced them, but I did not see them," he explains.

"I began to recite from the Qur'an, chapter one hundred and twelve. You know it."

Together we recited in Arabic:

'Qul huwa ALLAHu Ahud; ALLAHu Samad. Lam ya lid; wa lam yu lud. Wa lam yakun lahu kufuwan Ahud.'

"The Unity; The Sincerity"
Say: He is Allah, the One and Only; Allah,
the Eternal, Absolute; He begetteth not,
nor is He begotten; And
there is none like unto Him.
The Qur'an 112

"I prayed these verses seven times," he continues; "I was surrounded in bright, white, angelic lights. When I was able to distinguish the faces of these rebels again they were putting down their weapons."

The Chief tells how he questioned the assassins as to why they had come. They told him they didn't know why. That evening he tells me, we sat and talked as father to sons. Each of the remaining assassins reclaimed there faith by reciting,

'La elaa ha el 'llah; Muhammadur rasoolulah'
"There is no deity, accept ALLAH; and Muhammad is his messenger."

"Sheikh Ali-Salaam," he says, "Never let anyone influence you to doubt your faith; ALLAH is real and answers the believer."

from the records, Ali-Salaam

But I say unto you, Love your enemies, bless them that curse you, do good to them that hate you, and pray for them which despitefully use you, and persecute you;
The New Testament, Matthew 5:44

"It may be that God will grant love (and friendship) between you and those whom ye (now) hold as enemies...God forbids you not, with regard to those who fight you not for (your) faith nor drive you out of your homes, from dealing kindly and justly with them, for God loveth those who are just."
The Qur'an 60:7-8

I had the privilede to hear Mr. Ali-Salaam speak before tens of thousands while visitng Seattle recently...His sincere conviction and vision for humanity is readily apparent. He was as dynamic in person as his words are on the printed page.

ETHAN RYEBACH, SYDNEY, AUSTRALIA

Ali-Salaam is available for keynote presentations, booksignings, seminars and workshops.

Learn more by visiting
www.ali-salaam.com

KEYNOTE PRESENTATION
inquiries can be sent to
info@ali-salaam.com

Leadership for the New Millenium

Becoming Human; Being Human Seminar Series

"Jewish villages were built in the place of Arab villages. You do not even know the names of these Arab villages, and I do not blame you because geography books no longer exist, not only do the books not exist, the Arab villages are not there either. Nahlal arose in the place of Mahlul; Kibbutz Gvat in the place of Jibta; Kibbutz Sarid in the place of Huneifis; and Kefar Yehushu'a in the place of Tal al-Shuman. There is not one single place built in this country that did not have a former Arab population."

Moshe Dayan addressing the Technion (Israel Institute of Technology), Haifa (as quoted in Ha'aretz, 4 April 1969).

Ta'ayush ~ Living Together

Eight thousand Arab Israelis live in Issawiya; a village in northeast Jerusalem adjacent to the French Hill. Nearby is a campus, Hebrew University. The residents here carry special blue identity cards confirming their ethnicity as Palestinian or Arab; a unique class of Israeli citizens. Many of these families have for generations, worked and paid their municipal taxes and receive virtually no services.

Men and women returning from work, university, medical check ups and other routine daily affairs have endured a month long blockade to the entrances of Issawiya. The police arbitrarily permit admittance; while most residents are forced to sleep in their cars or on the street.

On the eve of Yom Ha-Atzma'ut (Israeli Independence) the Israeli police escalate their intimidation of the citizens of Issawiya, randomly throwing tear gas and stun grenades; there is no evidence this force is necessary. Children playing in the streets of the village are targeted by the police.

The story of humiliation is being repeated in Arab villages throughout Israel, I am told this by Noa'. Noa's father is a retired Israeli army officer. Noa' grew up listening to accounts of 'patrols' such as these being exchanged in air of pride at family gatherings. Now witnessing the atrocities she is ashamed, outraged, but most of all determined to take action against the injustices perpetrated on Israeli's 'blue class citizens'. Noa' is becoming human; her nationality and ethnicity does not blind her to the evils that are Israel's dark secret from the world.

Noa' is a member of an organization called Ta'ayush; an Arabic word meaning living together. Noa' and I met at the home of a colleague. Together we are part of a northwest effort called the 'Good Dialogue'. Our objective is to stimulate discussion among Palestinians and Israelis that one day may change international policies in the Middle East to policies that are fair and just to all the citizens of Israel, Gaza, the West Bank and in the occupied territories.

Noa's companion is a twenty-two year old woman named Leena. Leena is an Israeli *'citizen'*; she is ethnically Palestinian and also a member of Ta'ayush. She explains that their organization is an association of direct action, it was established at the early stages of the second Intifada, after the tragic events of

October 2000, in which Israeli police killed twelve Israeli Arabs.

Leena, Noa and the hundreds of other Ta'ayushim (*Ta'ayush members*) are hopeful for the future of Israel and Palestine. They are taking action to end what they termed 'Apartheid' in Israel. They are emphatic as they tell me that Americans would never accept the ethnic segregation and racist discrimination that exists within Israel. The Ta'ayushim have developed forms of Arab-Jewish nonviolent action at the grass-roots level in Israel itself and in the *Occupied Territories*.

"I never knew Arabs prior to joining Ta'ayush," Noa' explains. "Now together we have embraced, laughed and cried, but most importantly we work together to end the cycle of brutality in our country."

On another occasion outside Issawiya, more than three hundred men were stranded outside of their barricaded village for days. Several dozen Ta'ayushim joined the displaced villagers bringing blankets and food. Inspections by a dozen members able to sneak inside, reported that major damage was inflicted on several businesses. The site looked as if a major battle had taken place there, although it had actually been empty. In some instances the owners opened the businesses for inspection by the security forces. The police would then blow up the rear door of the shops in order to enter a small courtyard in the rear. They unnecessarily destroyed valuable items and pilfered others for personal gain.

This is an all too familiar scene as these types of tactics are similar to the ones employed by the Israeli military in Balata and other refugee camps.

As I observe this twenty-year old woman, I am impressed by her courage and conviction. One day she was among several hundred of the Ta'ayushim who returned to Issawiya and took apart the barricade to the village.

"This was my most serious run in with the police." Noa' told me.

Many of her colleagues had to be hospitalized and others were arrested. Often the police try to single out the Arabs among the Ta'ayushim but the members make it as difficult as possible. On several occasions Israeli Ta'ayushim placed their bodies beneath the wheels of military and police vehicles.

Noa' and Leena are currently in North America speaking wherever they can to raise awareness of the realities in Israel and to present the work of Ta'ayush.

A ray of light in the darkness, these Christians, Jews, Muslims, Palestinians and Israelis, whose faith in humanity and the right to life with dignity for all, have persevered, while risking their lives for justice.

Leena states, "This is about getting to know the human being. We have participated in paving roads, setting up playgrounds, planting trees throughout Israel and in the West Bank."

The friendship between Leena and Noa' is genuine. They will continue to participate in organizing convoys of food, medicine, and other necessities to besieged Palestinian towns and refugee camps (including Jenin), and also work to stop the expulsion of Palestinians from South Hebron.

In addition, many of Ta'ayush's activities involve working for equality between all Israeli citizens within Israel. Leena Dallasheh and Noa Nativ will speak about the ways Israelis and Palestinians can live and work together in peace.

They are being human sharing their lives, risking their lives because they believe in life, liberty and the pursuit of happiness and justice for all.

I can unequivocally state that not a single Palestinian should lose their life, dignity or property again; through the horrific and unjust acts done in the name of Israeli security. I am equally as certain that not another child, woman or man should lose their life through the condemnable act of someone strapping on a bomb violating their life and others in the name of Palestinian liberation.

The transgression of these people upon one another needs to give way to understanding, forgiveness and reconciliation.

Perhaps others will learn from the compassionate human efforts of these two young women of disparate cultures. Perhaps hate will be set aside for justice and equity. Perhaps despair will be overcome by kindness and hope can be born of the tragedies of the Children of Abraham. We must pray and act.

~ Ali-Salaam ~

Say: I seek refuge with the Lord and Cherisher of Mankind, The King (or Ruler) of Mankind, The GOD (or judge) of Mankind, From the evil of the sneaking whisperer, (The same) who whispers into the hearts of Mankind,- Of the jinn and of mankind.

The Qur'an, The Final Chapter (114)

"To sin by silence when they should
protest makes cowards of men"
President Abraham Lincoln

A Stand for Justice

On Sunday, June 10, 2002, about 100 people from four British Judo Clubs attended a ?friendly? match alongside several French judo clubs near Paris.

All was proceeding well; children and youth from the British teams had won over 35 medals; everyone was enjoying the day.

Then, a ten year old competitor on a British team was forbidden from taking part in the match. Why? Because this young girl Zainab wore a traditional Muslim head covering along with her judo uniform. If she would remove the head covering, she would be allowed to play.

Leigh Davies, of the Willesden Judo Club, protested the French ruling, but to no avail. When Leigh called on the British contingent to walk out, all one hundred did so immediately. Without being told to do so, the children and youth who had played and won, began to renounce their medals to the French hosts.

Afterwards I asked children how they felt about walking out of the match, and returning their hard-earned medals. The children referred to how angry they were by the way Zainab had been treated. They kept asking, why would someone be kept from a game just because she follows her religion by wearing a head covering? Many said that they never want to see that kind of people again. Repeatedly, children said they were proud of Zainab for taking a stand for what she believes in.

In turn, I am extremely proud of all the one hundred people from the British team, children and adults, who stood beside Zainab. They are of many races and religions, but they are united in their respect for sport and for fair play.

I am Zainab's Mom.

I am asking each of you to write to Leigh Davies of Willesden Judo Club, the person that initiated this demonstration of justice.

Even if only in a few words, please take the time out to show gratitude and appreciation.

This brave and forceful stand taken by so many people on behalf of fair play and justice should not pass by, without the acknowledgment it deserves.

Dear Reader you may email to:
leighdavies@willesdenjudo.freeserve.co.uk

Let not mercy and truth forsake thee: bind them about thy neck; write them upon the table of thine heart.
Proverbs 3:3

Be Human

Becoming human is to find no esteem in superiority;

Being human is gratefulness, humility and willingness to accept the miracle that is you and me.

Becoming human is to understand that guilt and innocence are subjective to our experience and that history is subjective to our perspective.

Being human is to bring relief to our common experience.

Becoming human is not the freedom to say and do whatever you want; but rather the freedom to refrain from acts that injure the heart of others.

Being human is freeing the slave, nourishing our young, foregoing ignorance, choosing life.

Becoming human is having the courage to always seek justice, justice for all.

Being human is being just, and the compassion of the just overrides their own desires.

Becoming human is to voice the silent echoes of the heart; and light the path of justice with words of truth and hope.

Being human is to know the value of each in every member of humanity; and stand patient and firm for their dignity.

Becoming human is to know that each breath brings

each of us closer to the change called death; our life's rhythm is best expressed through our sublime kinship with all that exists.

Being human is to marvel at the engineering ingenuity of the ant and bee; and gaze to the starlit heavens with wonder.

Becoming human is a miraculous journey where you need only to be ordinary to undertake.

Becoming human is to grieve in desperation for dignity.

Being human is to abstain from desperate actions.

Becoming human is to protest and endure the misery of oppression.

Being human is to value life and never to be the oppressor.

Becoming human is to face the rage of tyrants or live in a state of tyranny.

Being Human is to endure with valor, and teared eyes; with a still loving soul.

Becoming human is to need, and long for companionship;

Being human is to be needed.

Becoming human is to vision and dream.

Being human is a poetic empathic intimacy; sublime and surreal.

Becoming human is to contemplate and ponder the mysteries of space time and the origination of existence.

Being human is the simple charity of a smile or a gentle greeting to a passerby.

Becoming human is to accept our strengths and weaknesses as who we are.

Being human is to accept and love others as they are.

Becoming human is embracing one another, each with our weaknesses and strengths, because we all have a need to belong.

Becoming human is to be aching with love, relinquishing fear and working together.

Becoming human is to recognize that the profits of war profits no one and mankind must cease its inhumanity to man.

from the records, Ali-Salaam

"The sea-shore is a sort of neutral ground, a most advantageous point from which to contemplate this world.."

Henry David Thoreau

From Sea to Shining Sea

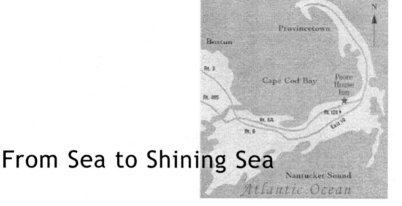

Green Harbor to the Mediterranean

As a boy I would run into the frigid waters of the North Atlantic Ocean. Before it reached my knee I would turn and run squealing back to the white sands of Green Harbor.

As a youth I was much too macho to do that. I learned to enjoy the frigid waters body surfing with my peers for hours, inducing low grade hypothermia upon myself; solidifying my position as a solitary alpha male. The beach was the place to hang out for the young people living in the picturesque suburbs on the South Shore of Massachusetts; parochial towns rich in national history. The Pilgrims landing at Plymouth Rock on the Mayflower, the First Thanksgiving dinner and the Boston Tea Party, indeed, the Slave Trade, the Revolutionary War, and the Kennedy's are all part of the high-priced historical allure of these places. Weymouth Landing, World's End; Plymouth Bay to Provincetown at the tip of Cape Cod; these suburban towns and ocean shores are the settings of my youthful excursions.

As a melancholy young man, I would often sit alone among the rocks and look upon the choppy murky waves from mid-afternoon to dusk; my classmates nearby on the beach. The buzz of their conversation and laughter is faintly carried on the wind to my isolated perch.

The hypnotic motion of the waves allows me to let my mind float adrift upon the sea of time. The northeast winds and fragrant salt air carry my thoughts across the bow of the present to the stern of the past. I envision my paternal ancestors' rugged merchant mariners and whalers not intimidated by the unfriendly and often hostile waters of the Atlantic.

Gazing on the golden horizon where the sky meets the sea, I am transformed beyond the limits of my body from the rocky isthmus jutting out into the New England coast line. Free from my body I travel beyond the limits of time and space. Soon, I am sitting high upon *Jabal Tarek* (the Rock of Gibraltar). It is the eighth century AD, I am alive in an ancient age. These pages of history were swept from the world history taught in my secondary school. In this enlightened age my paternal ancestors are the noble rulers of Al Andalus (Andalusia); the Moors of Spain.

My surreal journey is beyond the skein of linear time. I am in awe of the human cooperation of Muslims, Christians and Jews. Europeans, Arabs, Asians and Africans contribute to the scientific, cultural and intellectual growth of mankind. At the speed of light I pass through the centuries. I soar through the fragrant orange and olive groves of the Sierra Nevada; my spirit soars higher and I can see the grandeur of Granada homes; fourteenth century palaces of the Moorish kings. I can see clearly the images of Alhambra; its majestic towers, elaborate mosaics and ornately decorated rooms.

I continue on to Cordoba and Seville, cities with azure and topaz jeweled skies, lush gardens and ornate fountains; there are pools, pavilions, majestic masjids and universities; the height of culture and education centered on the Iberian Peninsula. Al Andalus brought Europe from the Dark Ages to its Renaissance. The words written by Victor Robinson in his "Story of Medicine" whispers in the recesses of my memory:

"Europe was dark at sunset, Cordoba shone with public lamps; Europe was dirty, Cordoba built a thousand baths; Europe was covered with vermin, Cordoba changed its undergarments daily; Europe lay in mud, Cordoba streets were paved; Europe's palaces had smoke-holes in the ceiling, Cordoba's arabesques were exquisite; Europe's nobility could not sign its name, Cordoba's children went to school; Europe's monks could not read the baptismal service, Cordoba's teachers created a library of Alexandrine dimensions."

'Mankind again is moving toward the darkest of ages,' I thought. The white foamy waves of the ocean thunderously crash against the rocks, momentarily stirring analytical thoughts.

Dungeons and a Long Rocky Beach

Still, entranced with the motions of the waves my mind drifts again in time; I thought of my maternal ancestors who suffered a fate no less then Hitler's

Holocaust in dark dungeons and pits. Their dismal abode beneath the fertile West African earth; perhaps beneath present day Ghana or Senegal or the more infamous *'Point of No Return'* at Gberefu Island or the nearby port of Badagary in Nigeria.

The nameless faces of the hundreds of thousands of my forefathers who suffered and expired in the despicable conditions of what the British cruelly misnamed Cape Coast Castle; in reality it was *the Auschwitz of Africa*. A concentration camp veiled as a place of commerce presided over by the British during the peak of the slave trade in the 1700's. At Cape Coast Castle, men women and children were thrown into an abyss of hot dungeons, where they would reside for months living in the filth of their own waste. Reduced to delirium and forced to inflict harm on one another in a fight for survival over the meager food and water provisions supplied to them.

Countless hours bound in solitary confinement; buried alive. I shudder and feel nauseous as I recall how meager morsels of food and water were dumped through a small hole in the top of these captives' prison-crypt. In these wretched conditions my maternal ancestors ate, drank, vomited, urinated, defecated, and slept. I am not sure if it is the chilled salt air of the sea or the anguish of their ancient souls that cause these tears to fall from my eyes.

The Dutch traders were not to be out done by the British. Elmina Castle's infamous female dungeons would rival any German *'detention center'*. Elmina Castle was a stronghold of dungeons and pits of despair for my helpless captive maternal ancestors.

Outside the dungeons across the courtyard was a church where this European Gestapo ironically, prayed. In the courtyard was a cell reserved for warrior prisoners who rebelled. Condemned to death by a kangaroo court; they were left to an excruciating death of starvation. The shrieking anguish of these vanquished warriors sent notice to others that valor and bravery at Elmina Castle was a vice.

The European captors masquerading as gentleman officers often raped the mothers of humanity. Their preying eyes would inspect their victims from a balcony as the captive women were displayed in the courtyard below. The selected victim would be roughly and immodestly washed and then shoved through a door into an adjacent room where she would be repeatedly raped. If by misfortune she became pregnant, she was set free to remain in Africa; her body imprisoned with the fruit of her oppressors' dastardly deed.

The surviving captives would leave the pits only to be blinded and have there naked bodies scorched by the fierce equatorial sun as they were transferred to the putrid and miserable bowels of a slave ship. Shackled and chained in a hell, fueled by man's malevolent inhumanity to mankind.

Wretchedly and pitifully these twice victimized members of humanity endured another dark stinking imprisonment. Suffering first as the losers in warfare, and then to be traded or sold to an even greater more insufferable enemy.

Sadly I contemplate how hundreds of thousands of my maternal ancestors' corpses were destined to be food for the creatures of the Atlantic's deep frigid waters. Others to survive the nightmare only to slave in the sugar cane fields in the Isles of the West Indies.

The high winds brought the ocean waters crashing down on the rocky New England coast line. The thundering roar shocked me back to the present. The late afternoon had faded into night, barefoot; I stealthily navigated a judicious course back along the narrow isthmus of jagged rocks to rejoin my senior classmates. They were still sitting in a circle upon the sands indulging on what President Clinton didn't inhale. I found a solitary spot amongst them. I watched as the joint passed over my classmate Jerry several times.

"What am I black," he exclaimed!

I guess the deepness of the night rendered me invisible in their midst. In awkward silence followed as they became aware of my presence . I slipped away again to my familiar perch on one of the rocky prominences jutting out from the Massachusetts coastline.

It was not the sweet pungent fragrance of cannabis that expanded my mind. I am grateful for the chilled early summer night and balmy winds and fragrance of the sea releasing me from my body.

I look upon the water, allowing my being to synchronize with the ocean's rhythm; my spirit soaring three thousand miles across the farthest reaches of the world's second largest ocean, this time to the shores of Africa.

We are living in a dark age. Perhaps as in the ancestral home of my forefathers a second renaissance would take place. Perhaps there I would be more than just 'black'. I would be a person, a human being whose cultural and history had meaning. Africa richest in world resources could rediscover it's lost history and I could wash the wounds of bigotry and hatred from my spirit. One day by the will of the Supreme Divinity, I hope to return to the homelands of my forefather's body, mind and rejuvenated soul.

A wave crashes heavily over the rocks drenching me in the spray. I need to return home by eleven.

> The history of an oppressed people is hidden in the lies and the agreed myth of its conquerors.
> *Meridel Le Sueur*

The Other Shore

Sierra Leone is a small beautiful West African country. Three thousand feet above sea level and projecting into the Atlantic Ocean are the Peninsula Mountains, which extend nearly twenty miles from the city of Freetown. From coastal sandy beaches to the uppermost point of the Peninsula Mountains, the vegetation progressively transforms from small sand binders at the beach side to a coastal savanna with mangroves, and then to dense tropical forests at the mountain slopes. It is to the valley of one of these mountains I must travel if our aid mission is to be successful. My travel companion is Greg, a Pentecostal Christian. We are two men of different belief systems; but our faith makes us believe that we can make a difference.

Freetown, the capital city of the country has a natural harbor that serves as the central port for many ocean vessels in the region. During World Wars I and II it was strategically important as a naval base for British soldiers.

It was two o'clock in the morning when our plane landed at Lungi International Airport outside the city on the shores of a small Atlantic inlet. Three decades had passed since my reflective ruminations on the Atlantic beaches of Massachusetts. I had finally crossed the great sea to my maternal ancestral homeland. I return finally with my Anglo companion on a humble mission of mercy. In the northern provinces of the country the people are facing certain famine. Eleven years of brutal war has destroyed lives and farm lands. Seed stores have been torched as well as masjids (mosques) schools and homes. Our mission is to purchase and deliver eight hundred, fifty kilogram bags of rice. This staple food by ALLAH's mercy, will prevent a food crisis for the people of the Wara Wara Bofodea Chiefdom. By ALLAH's grace the fragile peace will remain and next year the people will be able to resume planting and moving towards self-sufficiency.

There was still a helicopter to catch to Freetown, first place in the British Colonies where the slave trade had been outlawed, an appropriate place for my return. It is a brief fifteen minutes across the Lungi inlet. The chopper settles down on the sandy beach of the Atlantic on the outskirts of Freetown, Sierra Leone.

Adrenaline pours through me. I exit the craft with my companion and less than two dozen other passengers. Oblivious to them I knelt in the sands and rub it over my face and limbs in dry ablution; I prostrate my forehead and face in the sandy red earth; my heart cries out in glory to the Immortal Divinity (ALLAH) for granting my almost forgotten prayer.

"Human beings are so made that the ones who do the crushing feel nothing; it is the person crushed who feels what is happening. Unless one has placed oneself on the side of the oppressed, to feel with them, one cannot understand."   *Simone Weil*

Freetown

Our gracious host Kamara arrives with a car and security to take us to our lodgings in Freetown. My first view of the city is in the shadowy depths of the African night skies. In the night Freetown is eerie and austere. We arrive at a mission house on Colt Farm Road.

Our abode is in the section of the city scheduled for a roving black out. Disheveled and thoroughly travel worn, I am concerned as I watch our house sitter, Moses, fiddle with the padlocks and heavy chains on the gate. A knot of fear forms in my stomach. I wonder just how much risk there is going to be on this mission. I gather my two bags, politely refuse my hosts assistance and trudge up the dark concrete stairs to the second level of the mission house.

By candle light Moses shows us to our respective sleeping quarters and the bathroom. Seeing the plumbing fixtures I feel relief; and then dismay when I find out due to necessity they are mere semi-functional ornamentation.

Travel exhaustion permits me to find two hours of restless slumber in the *'cool'* evening air of eighty-five degrees and only ninety percent humidity. A thought comes to mind, eat as little as possible and avoid using the *facilities*. This certainly is going to be an experience for *a 'suburbanite Moorish prince.'* I force my mental voice to keep quiet so I can get some sleep.

A cool breeze from the ocean caresses my consciousness. Alhumdulilah *(Praise GOD)*! I hear a faint but distinct call of ALLAHu Akbar *(GOD is Great)* riding the winds. My heart leaps and I sit up, gathering my single white sheet, and drawing it about me as a cloak, I peer out through the wrought iron window grids. Again, again and again the faint verse of the Adhan *(the Islamic call to prayer)* graces my ears. It seems to be coming from the distant hills in the northwest. I can not make out any sign of a minaret *(prayer tower)*.

ALLAHu Akbar, ALLAHu Akbar rides upon the winds, this time stronger and more powerful. It is a different voice and I began to notice faint flickering of lights approximately midway from my quarters to the farthest hillside to the northwest, perhaps a mile to the west. The early dawn sky seems dark. I gather the sheet more tightly around me and rush down the corridor to the living room and out on to the balcony that faces east towards the ocean.

I am awestruck by the vivid hues of the dawn skies as the sun was beginning its rise over the ocean waters. In the west the sky is still dark and ornamented with lights of antiquity from thousands upon thousands of celestial bodies. The date palms again mercifully swept an ocean breeze across Freetown. *Alhumdulilah!*

Ebullient, I raise my hands drawing deep breaths; eyes-wide in amazement, I lightly dance a solitary dance under the beauty of ancestral skies. Again, ALLAHu Akbar shatters the early morning air. I realize that this is a third voice; there must be many masjids in this vicinity. Bending down I gather the sheet around to regain my modesty, and dash back through the darkness and quiet of the mission house to my quarters.

Out the window below a myriad of candle lights cast shadows revealing a refugee shanty encampment. I see deep images moving about. Straining my eyes I can not see the masjid *(mosque)*. Hastily I make my wudu *(ritual washing)*, dress and rush through the corridor, down the stairs groping my way in the early morning darkness. I am anxious to follow the sound of the Adhan *(call to prayer)* and to make my way to congregational prayer; it would be my first ever in Africa.

I reach the front gate to find it chained and locked. Looking at the height I quickly decide that I would have to take my five foot eleven, two hundred twenty pound frame and squeeze under the gate. To my amazement I accomplished the task. Dusting myself off I follow the sound of the call to prayer.

Hi Yah Ala Falah *(Come to Success)* I made my way ten yards down a very uneven rocky path. Hi Yah Ala Falah. I stumble forward for twenty yards and begin to notice dark eyes among the morning shadows staring at the stranger.

As Salatul Khairum Minal Nawm *(Prayer is Better than sleep)*. I turned left and amble my way up another narrow passage inclining upward. About forty yards in the distance I saw the reflection of a white thobe *(prayer gown)* and moved quickly toward it. Suddenly it moves left and again I am momentarily lost in the early morning darkness.

As Salatul Khairum Minal Nawm, exclaims the

Muezzin (*the caller for prayer*). I stub my toe as I abruptly come upon crudely roughed out earthen steps in the path.

ALLAHu Akbar, ALLAHu Akbar, the Muezzin calls. I am very close; I glance left and notice a shadowy parade of people just ten yards away. I close the gap and follow.

La elaa ha el'llah, *(There is no Deity, accept ALLAH)*. The last line of the Adhan reaches me as I remove my flats and cross the stone carved threshold into the candle lit masjid.

Alhumdulilah, my heart is joyous as I take my place, shoulder to shoulder, foot to foot amongst my brethren in the prayer line.

The Road to Kabala

The urgent need of our journey was to deliver eighty thousand kilograms of rice to the people of Wara Wara Bofodea Chiefdom in the northern provinces of Sierra Leone near the Guinea border. The Chiefdom of twenty-five thousand plus people were among the most victimized people of the brutal and horrific eleven year war. Seventy thousand citizens had fled and now live in camps in various cities throughout the country and in neighboring Guinea.

It would take several days for my Christian companion to complete the monetary exchange and negotiate a wholesale purchase of rice from the Lebanese importers at the port. He would also have to negotiate through Major Padre' Kargbo, a war veteran and military chaplain for transport and escort for our journey to Bofodea Chiefdom. There is an unspoken theme of redemption and atonement for Greg and myself on this humanitarian mission. A Christian and a Muslim together praying and hoping to help those in dire need; perhaps Mediterranean winds of ancient Andalusia have passed through the gates of time, and arrived here in Sierra Leone.

In order to deliver the rice needed to save lives of the people of Bofodea, we must take the road to Kabala. The road to Kabala will be a journey that I could not have ever anticipated. Our small convoy of three army cargo transports and one Toyota Land Rover will have to complete the hundred and fifty mile trek to Kabala and then off load to other vehicles and then continue on to Bofodea. The first leg of this journey should take five hours, in reality it would take nine hours. The deteriorated conditions of the roads are beyond the imagination of this suburbanite.

Dressed in sandals, khakis and an Australian safari hat and with my black Egyptian cotton prayer turban serving as a hat band, I climb aboard the Land Rover. I sit precariously at the rear end of the vehicle *'sardine style'*. Clearly the seven passengers, their luggage and musical instruments are far above the intended capacity of this vehicle. My coccyx learns to endure abuse reminiscent of my first learning to ride a horse in the White Mountains of New England.

It would take one hour for our convoy to wind its way from the port of Freetown through the endless stream of human retailers crowding the narrow streets. Everyone in Freetown is a retailer, wares arranging from a single stick of gum, baggies of frozen water, sweat cloths, food stuffs and other miscellaneous sundries. Sierra Leonean people are patient; enduring the one hundred ten degree heat with ninety percent humidity for twelve hours in order to perhaps earn a dollar by days end.

Our military drivers carefully urge our convoy through the human masses until we reach the road from Freetown to Kabala. Dusk is settling in as we reach the outskirts of the city. We only need to make one quick pit stop to top off our petrol and purchase some provisions for the journey. As we pull into the station retailers of all ages descend upon us selling literally *'daily bread'*. My hosts handle the negotiations and purchases. After much hand reaching and squeezing, a half dozen whole loaves of white bread are purchased along with a case of bottled water for a sum less than five dollars.

Night falls quickly in equatorial West Africa. Star light and headlights cast languid shadows. Wind whips through the Land Rover at first cooling, but it is not long before I am painfully aware of the red clay sands from the unpaved road biting my face. I remove the prayer turban wrapped around my hat and mask myself fully covering my face. I do my best to ride the waves of jostles, thuds and bumps as the other members of our convoy converse in their native Creole.

We first travel south as one of my companions now and then informs me of the upcoming towns or villages first comes Wellington, Hastings, Waterloo and then Songo. At the village of Songo we begin a more direct route to Kabala traveling northwest. All of these places appear the same in the evening darkness. Cement or clay buildings close to the roadway with many people chatting and selling by candle light. Dark shiny faces accustomed to the humidity and oppressive heat.

We pass through Lunsar and bypass Makeni. Makeni was the rebel capital during the height of the war and though peace and the continued hope of peace seems to be in everyone's heart; it is clear that our security chief Mansueray feels *'caution is the better part of valor.'* After two hours we stop to *'ease'* ourselves at Bumbuna, it is the first place that Mansueray feels comfortable enough for us to stop.

Our little convoy is conspicuous and our cargo represents significant wealth for a people impoverished and facing famine as a result of the ravages of war. The now familiar vendors approach as we awkwardly disembark from the crowded Land Rover; desperately hoping that we might desire a mango, piece of gum or some local cuisine prepared by the side of the road. In my suburban naiveté I ask Mansueray where I can relieve myself; he smiles, crow's feet at the corners of his eyes etch themselves in his deep ebony skin; with a twinkle in his eyes, Mansueray gestures off to side of the road and says;

"Where ever you like."

After a short time, members of our party reappear

one by one from various shadowy places to again situate themselves in our transport. Only ninety miles and *'who knows'* how many hours to go before we reach Kabala, which I am to understand is one of the outstanding cities of the country.

I learn that before the war, the Northern provinces with Kabala as their center of commerce; provided sixty percent of the agricultural produce to the country and forty percent of the meat products. It is clear to me that all of my hosts and guides are fond and proud of that place.

We continued on through Bumbuna and passed through Bendugu. Suddenly, Chapman one of our military escorts shouts for our driver to stop; Mansueray agrees. We halt as they both hastily leap from the vehicle and trek back about forty yards. They are inspecting something in the road; they turn it over several times examining it carefully. Chapman begins to search through the high grasses several minutes while Mansueray picks up the obviously dead animal by the tail. It appears to be some type of large rodent. He places it between his feet and mine as he climbs in. Chapman resumes his precarious perch in a semi-squat, feet resting on the bumper and hands grasping the upper rear row bar. He informs our group there are no more of the creatures to be found. Cringing, I think, Ya ALLAH *(My GOD)* with a silent sigh of relief. Gears grind and engines roar as our convoy moves out again.

We pass through Bendugu to Alikailia; here we begin to travel due north; for the final sixty miles to Kabala. I find myself anxious to reach this place. I am anticipating that I will finally see a place with the familiar pristine finishes of American suburbs which I had come to take for granted. Half way between Alikailia and Kabala, my companions and I have grown noticeably weary of this arduous ride. The drivers are exhausted and there is concern for the trailing truck in the convoy, which we have not seen for some time. There is unspoken fear and subdue silence as we delay for several minutes hoping they will catch up. We continue on for another thirty minutes. Our driver pulls into a rest area or so it seemed, in short order Mansueray stated that he was not comfortable with our resting here. He instructed the drivers to continue all the way to Kabala and hope that the missing vehicle arrives after us.

The muscles in my back are aching from a culmination of the jarring and slamming of the transport through the pot craters *(pot holes would be a gross under statement)* on the road to Kabala. My arm is weary from the tense grip on the vertical row bar at the rear of the Land Rover for the past five hours, in a meager attempt to reduce the crashing of my head against the upper row bars. The final miles seem uneventful except for my minds excruciating calculations of my physical discomforts.

In Sierra Leone *'comfort and convenience are not an option'*.

We arrive in Kabala in the pre dawn hours around two o'clock; still short one vehicle and its passengers. In the starlit early morning, I immediately recognize that Kabala's visual landscape is much the same as all other places in Sierra Leone. Every building appears forlorn and drab in need of some maintenance or constructive repair; my mental illusion of modern storefronts, chrome and glass is shattered.

Kabala was the first major city hit hard by the rebel soldiers. There is no hotel, motel, rooming house or convenient public shower. There would be no sleep tonight unless I opt to sleep sitting up with the dead rodent beneath my feet. I am motivated to exit the transport stiffly, gingerly watching my step. I follow my hosts who are making their way across the dusty parking lot to the roaring sound of cheers at an athletic event. I quickly catch up as they pass through the gates of a Sierra Leone Discothèque complete with satellite television.

It's World Cup opening rounds and football (soccer to us Americans) is the sporting love of Africa. We spend the remainder of the evening in semiconsciousness rehydrating ourselves on Fanta or Malta and rooting for Cameroon; Africa's best hope in this world tournament.

One of my hosts, Kamara, has a home in Kabala and is a Member of Parliament. He sends word for his family to prepare breakfast for our travel worn troop. By seven the next morning, the sun is burning bright in clear skies. This is the rainy season but there is not a hint that a desired deluge of waters will grace us with its presence.

Breakfast is a steamy hot plate of rice and meat. I decline and forswear that I am not hungry. I do accept a bottle of water eagerly. As the men gather around on the porch eating from a single large plate, Moses and the other members of the missing crew appear with our driver to everyone's relief. I learn that our driver, a former child-rebel soldier turned man had retraced our route. Eventually he had found the missing vehicle broken down by the side of the road with a flat. They had somehow found a suitable repair in the middle of nowhere and had arrived in Kabala a *mere five hours later.*

Arrangements have to be made for other vehicles. The military trucks are too heavy and wide to negotiate the road to the Wara Wara Bofodea Chiefdom. I am astounded to learn that the roads can get worse. Kamara being the consummate politician will manage acquiring a truck through prudent negotiations with state officials and the local police. It will require that some of our cargo remain in Kabala.

It soon becomes apparent that with only thirty-two miles to go we will not depart for our ultimate destination until late afternoon. I decide to take a walk with Mansueray who is a most affable gentleman of noble character that belies his profession as a government intelligence/security officer.

We walk the streets at an equatorial African pace which I estimate to be about one mile per hour. In such extreme heat you do not sweat salt; you sweat glucose. The perspiration on my hands is as thick as honey. As we exchange stories about our respective homes I am touched by the fondness and genuine love that he expresses for his small beleaguered country. Sierra Leone is about the size of South Carolina, a small country of approximately five million people. Wealthy with resources, it is the regions perfect victim for others geopolitical agendas. In my heart I pray for a lasting peace and that these people are given a fair opportunity to reach their noble goals.

I am curious about the dead rodent and inquire of Mansueray about the name of the animal. He tells me that it is called *cut-the-grass*. I laugh and ask him seriously what is the name of the animal; seriously he says *cut-the-grass* because that's what it does. It consumes the high grasses that grow up on the edge of the road. I asked him what they did with the one he found last night secretly hoping that it had been picked up for the value of it's skin. My worse fears were realized as he smiled and said, *'Breakfast'*.

I am happy that I declined to partake of that meal. We continued to amble about the city center, my Australian safari hat pinpointing me as non-indigenous. Passersby are quick with a smile and greeting. I found this to be one of the pleasantries of Sierra Leone. People do not pass one another anytime of day without a respectful and pleasant greeting. It is hard to imagine any of them engaged in martial conflict.

We returned back at Kamara's just in time to enjoy fresh succulent mango and pineapple before departing. The soldiers have headed back to Freetown. One police truck had been loaded and the remaining bags of rice stored in Kamara's house. It will take three trips to transport it all safely to Bofodea. Satiated on the fresh fruit, a culinary delight that became my dietary staple, I again resumed my precarious seating at the rear of the Land Rover for the short thirty-two mile trip to Bofodea.

Wara Wara Mountain

I look forward to reaching Bofodea. I am anxious to meet strangers in the hope that our humanitarian efforts will be enough to relieve their suffering until the next planting season. My body aching my internal being is still set on western travel time. I imagine a brief journey that even by Sierra Leonean standards could only be sixty to ninety minutes at best. How wrong I am. There is ample time for contemplation and I think how Africa's suffering seems to be unending.

Since the slave trade and European colonization of this land and people, it seems to be forever in turmoil. The inhumanity inflicted upon the people of Africa by the European colonists has been replaced by indigenous tribal fighting and despot ruthless regimes playing out the same *'imperialist disease of the heart.'*

In this instance the brutal amputation of arms and limbs of more than twenty thousand people, and an onslaught upon one another aided by outside factions for control of diamond lands.

The decade of the nineties was an explosion of wealth and technological innovation in America this unprecedented explosion of human innovation bypassed the tiny country of Sierra Leone. The children here under the age of twelve, have only lived as victims to the oppressive equatorial heat under the even more oppressive tyranny of mankind's despicable greed and lust.

It is with a still melancholy heart that I continue on silently in anticipation to Bofodea. It is the twenty first century but we are still living in the Dark Ages. 'Yah ALLAH, what will change the condition of the people,' I ask myself; I know the answer *'that which they will change themselves.'*

"Because Allah will never change the grace which He hath bestowed on a people until they change what is in their (hearts) souls: and verily Allah is He Who hears and knows (all things)."   *The Qur'an 8:53*

    The final leg of our mission though only thirty-two miles is nearly equal in duration to the first one hundred sixty miles. The precarious road to Bofodea has two primary bridges and several small bridges that have deteriorated. This was the reason that we had to off load the rice from the larger military trucks in Kabala. The terrain is so rough it seems impassable. One violent jarring after another smashing my cranium against the Land Rover's upper row bars. Our overcrowded transport bottoms out in a crater masquerading as a pothole. The smashing of our bodies finally throws Chapman from his precarious perch of the rear bumper and another striking of my head on the row bars dislodges a porcelain filling from my upper left molar. I cling desperately to a row bar as the tailgate drops open.

    Miraculously our vehicle is still operable and it's passengers more or less intact. I remind myself that *'comfort and convenience are not an option'*. We continue bruised but whole to Bofodea.

Bofodea's remaining twenty five thousand residents are scattered in small villages throughout the cheifdom. Their schools, masjids and crops destroyed. Seeds for planting burned in their storehouses. The survivors are led by Sierra Leone's retired distinguished war hero. Paramount Chief Alimammy Hamidu. As we pass through several small compounds, naked children run after us waving with wide-eyed smiles and excited pointed gestures. I soon learn that it is the astonishing site of my companion Greg, a six foot-one three hundred pound white man. He is the equivalent of a world wonder to these isolated youngsters. As we wind our way deeper into the valley I catch glimpses of brilliantly colored tropical birds and an occasional small monkey.

After a treacherous four hour journey we arrive in Bofodea Township, nestled in a rich green fertile valley beneath Wara Wara Mountain.

Wara Wara Mountain is one of the country's largest and highest after Bintumani Peak which rises over six thousand feet above sea level. Chapman again still squatting dangerously off the rear bumper is very excited.

"This is my country, and I have never been this far before."

This seems incredible to me, Sierra Leone is about the size of South Carolina and this young military chaplain had never traveled this far within his homeland; whereas I have traveled to forty-nine of the fifty United States.

He exclaims, "Wow, look at that, I studied about this mountain in school, man and you came six thousand miles and you're seeing it too. Fantastic!"

Bofodea Township is precisely and efficiently planned; clearly defined earthen roads typical of a suburban plat absent the pavement and street lights; a positive contribution from a Wesleyan Methodist missionary. Our transport halts at a large cement home at the edge of town.

Here, nature's panoramic beauty is juxtaposed with the naked and poorly clothed children with swollen distended bellies; the results of eleven years of senseless strife and brutality.

Word quickly passes through the township announcing our arrival. Throngs of people in children gather in the front of the Chief's house as the band begins beating drums hailing our arrival. The youth receive instruction to off load the cargo vehicle so that it can return to reload in Kabala. Deftly, they place the heavy bags of rice on their heads and in parade like fashion carry them into the storehouse. They accomplish their task in a short time; throughout the afternoon into the next morning this activity is repeated until all five hundred fifty kilogram bags of rice are safely in storage.

The main purpose of our journey is completed. Alhumdulilah!

I truly share the experience of these elegant people's suffering as I am amongst them. Almost all of the elderly of the township are blind. Lack of proper medical treatment for maladies such as diabetes and cataracts are primary contributors to their condition. Medical care is virtually absent as a whole in Sierra Leone. These gentle wise souls travel about holding on to the end of a walking stick with two and three year-old children holding the other end, to guide them to the baths or wherever else they would like to go.

Several evenings I sat childlike at the elder's feet and listen intently to their hopes and dreams for their chiefdom and their country. The other men present range between the ages of twenty-one to forty. I am uplifted as they too, express their optimism and demonstrate their ability to forgive the past. Each of them begin and end there story with overwhelming expressions of gratitude for the delivery of rice. I am humbled; our aid seems so meager in light of the more devastating needs for a health care system, a revitalized educational system and capitol infrastructure.

The village children seem unaware of their abject poverty; they insist on having an all night celebration. They fire up the generator usually reserved for emergencies, string colored lights around the outdoor pavilion and lace large tropical tree fronds creating walls. I watch them smile, sing and dance with delight and gratefulness. They tell me how happy and amazed they are that someone from so far away could care about them.

Many of the children only know the pain and sorrow of their homeland. Most of their lives have been in struggle and fear from the RUF. Young children of Bofodea three and four years of age dance with coordination and rhythm beyond their years, beaming faces and white smiles and clear eyes full of genuine happiness. Adolescent and prepubescent alike release their anxieties in the shadows of torch lights and stars.

I am overwhelmed by their innocent beauty and joy.

Against the youngsters wishes, I politely retire to the front porch of Chief Alimammy's home where the elders have gathered talking in hushed tones and enjoying the cool mountain winds sweeping through the valley. I find a seat amongst the elders, who are almost invisible; their rich dark complexions melding in the deep evening shadows accented by meager candle light, punctuated by an occasional torch light of a neighbor passing by. I listen intently to the dark faces softly gleaming with perspiration. The depth of their sorrow and hopes could be seen even in the absence of incandescent light. In turn they talk of the war and its hardships. They do not have to add drama to the events. I find the malevolent brutality and butchering of mostly defenseless human beings unconscionable. Yet this had been their reality for more than a decade. The tragedies seem countless and the need overwhelming.

I am enlightened by my hosts, for with so little and amidst so much horror, their conversations turn to forgiveness, hope and renewal.

Sierra Leone has long been free of slavery. Perhaps now it has purged itself and is free of the greed that plagues all of humanity. There are no acts of vengeance and retaliation among the people. It is a country rich in resources and in spirit. Once this land was considered the Athens of Africa; perhaps now it could lead this continent and the world into a Renaissance that it so desperately needs.

The Beach

I am waiting for the helicopter to lift us to Lungi Airport across the bay to return to Europe. I leave my luggage at the heliport pavilion. The sound of the ocean beckons my spirit. I slip away from the crowd clamoring for tickets.

I slowly walk through the wet sands at the edge of the shore. The warm waters of the Atlantic wash against my ankles. I look upon the horizon line where the azure blue skies meet the aqua blue waters. The soft sound of the waves rolling in on the coastline is comforting, as is the strong ocean breeze bringing relief from the heat.

I stop and look upon the sea a familiar companion since my youth. The rhythm of the white capped waves washing over the shore stirs eclectic thoughts within me. There are gulls circling above, it appears they are moving inland. The winds are heavy and the skies are beginning to dim, a prelude to the first torrential downpour of the rainy season. As the weather is transformed so am I. It is time for my farewell prayer to Africa.

*'I pray that I have finally become human,
'wanting for others what I want for myself';
and that I can continue to be human,
doing unto others as I would have done for myself.
I silently ask the Sublime, Supreme Divinity to
show me the way to be of further service to
these wonderful people and all of mankind.
I know now, that upon returning home to
America I will have to share their sorrow
and tragedy; their dignity and hope
with as many people as I am able.
Omniscient, Bountiful Divinity You have inspired
the hearts of these people; through them
You have inspired me.
My brothers and sisters are filled with hope despite
all the bleakness about them.
The sharing of their lives with mine has given*

me more than I could ever give them.
Your bounty is endless; let me serve as a bearer of your gifts.'
Ameen.

Two men - one Christian, one Muslim; one of pale complexion, one with dark complexion landed on the Atlantic beaches of West Africa. We came on a simple mission to help feed the hungry, the least fortunate humans on earth. I know now that we must continue to help and encourage others to help; I am hoping and praying that by telling their story that the American people will respond with generosity. We can help the people of Sierra Leone regain their self sufficiency; restore their education and medical systems. I believe Inshaa ALLAH *(GOD willing)*, we will.

A thunder clap and the roar of the helicopter blades simultaneously interrupt my serene contemplation. The rains pour from the heavens and I am grateful for this heavenly shower; without haste I make my way back up to the heliport for the flight across the bay.

from the records, Ali-Salaam

Hast thou observed him who belieth religion? Then such is the (man) who repulses the orphan (with harshness), And encourages not the feeding of the needy. Ah, woe unto worshippers; Who are neglectful of their prayers, Who do (good) to be seen by men Yet refuse small kindnesses (and withhold the necessaries of life)! *The Qur'an, Chapter 107*

Rivalry in worldly increase distracteth you (abundance diverts you,) Until you come to the graves. *The Qur'an, 102: 1-2*

Praise ye the Lord: with my whole heart
I will God's praise declare, Where the
assemblies of the just and congregations
are.

The whole works of the Lord our God are
great above all measure, Sought out they
are of ev'ry one that doth therein take
pleasure.

His work most honourable is, most glorious
and pure, And his untainted righteousness
for ever doth endure.

His works most wonderful he hath made to
be thought upon: The Lord is gracious, and
he is full of compassion.

Psalms 111, 1-4

There is no freedom which is free
You pay the price right from the very start
Each one is measured by the strength
Of what he carries in his heart.

Everyone must have a distance. Everyone must run his own race. Though the sky is cold and cloudy; I feel the sunlight in my face.

In my life I've seen some changes; In my life I've felt some pain. But I've seen flowers on the hillside; Shining out in the pouring rain.

Author Unknown

Being human

Being human is to know that justice is not enforced by cruelty or military power, and sovereignty is not gained by the threat of mass destruction.

Becoming human is to hear the tormented cry out for peace.

Being human is to sow the seeds of forgiveness and reconciliation, water them with our word and deed; and patiently watch them grow.

Becoming human is to be human, to know tragedy and triumph, to wash the earth with our tears;

Being human is engaging life with the fullness of our heart and nurturing our souls existence in the light of one another's eyes.

Becoming human is imperfection mirrored in our experience.

Being human is discovering the victory in our mistakes. Our wisdom is gained through practice.

Becoming human is to recognize our created frailty and to be cognizant of this temporal existence; for this is at the heart of our desire to belong.

Being human is feeling our hearts in communion, free spirits clothed in the garments of culture, tradition, nations and religion.

Becoming human is not the sum of triumphs and victories, but the commitment and dedication that gifts them to our experience.

Being human is to know that there is finality to our mortal being.

Becoming human is the immortal moments of virtue that live in the hearts of those who have shown kindness and love.

Being human is to be truly human; learn to give, respect, honor and love while you can.

from the records, Ali-Salaam

LETTER OF JOHN PAUL II
TO ALL THE HEADS OF STATE AND GOVERNMENT
OF THE WORLD AND DECALOGUE OF ASSISI FOR PEACE

To Their Excellencies Heads of State or Government

A month ago, the Day of Prayer for Peace in the world took place in Assisi. Today my thoughts turn spontaneously to those responsible for the social and political life of the countries that were represented there by the religious authorities of many nations.

The inspired reflections of these men and women, representatives of different religious confessions, their sincere desire to work for peace, and their common quest for the true progress of the whole human family, found a sublime and yet concrete form in the "Decalogue" proclaimed at the end of this exceptional day.

I have the honour of presenting to Your Excellency the text of this common agreement, convinced that these ten propositions can inspire the political and social action of your government.

I observed that those who took part in the Assisi Meeting were more than ever motivated by a common conviction: humanity must choose between love and hatred. All of them, feeling that they belong to one and the same human family, were able to express their aspiration through these ten points, convinced that if hatred destroys, love, on the contrary, builds up.

I hope that the spirit and commitment of Assisi will lead all people of goodwill to seek truth, justice, freedom and love, so that every human person may enjoy his inalienable rights and every people, peace. For her part, the Catholic Church, who trusts and hopes in "the God of love and peace" (II Cor 13,11), will continue to work for loyal dialogue, reciprocal forgiveness and mutual harmony to clear the way for people in this third millennium.

With gratitude to Your Excellency, for the attention you will be kind enough to give my Message, I take the present opportunity offered to assure you of my prayerful best wishes.

From the Vatican, 24 February 2002.

Decalogue of Assisi for Peace

1. We commit ourselves to proclaiming our firm conviction that violence and terrorism are incompatible with the authentic spirit of religion, and, as we condemn every recourse to violence and war in the name of God or of religion, we commit ourselves to doing everything possible to eliminate the root causes of terrorism.

2. We commit ourselves to educating people to mutual respect and esteem, in order to help bring about a peaceful and fraternal coexistence between people of different ethnic groups, cultures and religions.

3. We commit ourselves to fostering the culture of dialogue, so that there will be an increase of understanding and mutual trust between individuals and among peoples, for these are the premise of authentic peace.

4. We commit ourselves to defending the right of everyone to live a decent life in accordance with their own cultural identity, and to form freely a family of his own.

5. We commit ourselves to frank and patient dialogue, refusing to consider our differences as an insurmountable barrier, but recognizing instead that to encounter the diversity of others can become an opportunity for greater reciprocal understanding.

6. We commit ourselves to forgiving one another

for past and present errors and prejudices, and to supporting one another in a common effort both to overcome selfishness and arrogance, hatred and violence, and to learn from the past that peace without justice is no true peace.

7. We commit ourselves to taking the side of the poor and the helpless, to speaking out for those who have no voice and to working effectively to change these situations, out of the conviction that no one can be happy alone.

8. We commit ourselves to taking up the cry of those who refuse to be resigned to violence and evil, and we are desire to make every effort possible to offer the men and women of our time real hope for justice and peace.

9. We commit ourselves to encouraging all efforts to promote friendship between peoples, for we are convinced that, in the absence of solidarity and understanding between peoples, technological progress exposes the world to a growing risk of destruction and death.

10. We commit ourselves to urging leaders of nations to make every effort to create and consolidate, on the national and international levels, a world of solidarity and peace based on justice.

" Iraqi children", Orlando Sentinel on March 2, 1999

The hospitals, devoid of almost everything they need, and staffed by doctors exhausted and grieving, are just a place to die for the thousands of Iraqi children suffering from diseases and infections brought on by the malnutrition and contaminated water. Our government is responsible for that. The embargo on Iraq, which even denies the Iraqis chlorine to use for purifying their water supply, has become a weapon of mass destruction. Half a million dead children — and that's a United Nations number — is mass destruction, I would say. Berrigan said in 1989 about 92 percent of the Iraqis had access to health care and that education was free through the university level. In that year, there was not a single case of cholera in the country. Today, there are thousands of cases — a direct result of contaminated water. There has been a fourfold increase in childhood leukemia, possibly linked to the depleted uranium the United States used in its shells.

Charley Reese

An Echo from the Drum of War

The war drum is beating in our land; as it did in Caesar's Rome' History unheeded; we will share the same ignoble fate of those before us.

I hear the drum of war; it is silencing the cries of the innocent; I am an American who can not keep silent while we lead the world on a reckless course.

The drum major is deaf from the resounding beat, the orchestra he can not hear!

The drum of war beats with a chaotic rhythm; out of time and syncopation; coercing an alliance of corrupted ideological miscegenation.

The drum of war echoes in my mind and brings only restless sleep, The drum of war plays an inane rhetorical symphony; it distorts the truth, and the reality of human needs.

If I were the drummer I would tare the skin from the kettle of the timpani, and free the muffled voices inside; I would listen to the echo from the drum of war.

Listen....

Osama's Letter

May ALLAH's peace be with you brother

With all my honor and open heart I send this message to you, my family and friends. The people in Iraq are angry and hurt in reaction to America attacking us. We ask ourselves; what is going on here in this world? We are people, we are human beings; does no one care about how we the Iraqi people are feeling?

Does no one care about the ills of our people; about what is happening to our country; its sufferance of hunger, destitution and sadness.

We are suffering from an eleven years siege that is imposed on our lovely country. The entire world knows what is happening in Iraq. We are devastated. Every year, one and a half million of our children, old people, and women are killed by disease and hunger; the same numbers of people will die next year.

We are already enduring a silent endless massacre from the United Nation's sanctions coerced by the United States and British Governments.

What will your next massacre to the Iraqi people bring? Will it bring anything other than more grief, agony and carnage to the people you purport to liberate?

How much more will our basic dignity and human

rights be violated by the world? Will you trade the red blood coursing through our bodies for the black oil streaming the bowels beneath the desert sands of our homeland?

As of now we receive medicine in which the dates are expired because the United Nation's sanctions delays deliveries to Iraq. Why; because maybe the medicines have chemical materials that could be used in chemical weapons. Instead of weapons taking lives, the atrocity of your sanctions do; the result is the same. Destitution gnaws the bones of the poor and makes life abysmal for the people of Iraq.

What do we expect from the next attack on Iraq; another war shown on the Big Screen of the World with the anesthetic reality of a video game.

What happens to us? What happens to our children, to old men and women, the sick and disabled? What happens to the people of Iraq?

In the USA, three thousand people died on the eleventh of September, this was tragic and our people were very sad. We know best the suffering of man's inhumanity to man.

Let me ask you this; what would you do if your family and your children and your lovely people were being attacked. Being attacked in their homes; attacked after all their years of suffering. Attacked though they are already weak and millions of souls lost each and every year, for more than a decade.

What if those one million persons were from your country? What would you be feeling? What would you do? Would you defend your beloved family and homeland?

Yet the world has already seen what America will do. One can only imagine the horror if a million American lives were lost. Would anyone in the world be safe? Others are accused of hijacking a religion for political gains. Who is hijacking peace and creating suffering in the name of protecting others?

We greet all the Americans who love the peace and support our cause and every cause of peace; and to all the Muslims who are bravely supporting us. Who love their brothers and sisters in Iraq; for this is the law of Islam *"Love your brother as yourself, want for others as you want for yourself."*

Here from Iraq, on behalf of my family and my people; we send our respect. But understand that despite all our suffering, despite the military supremacy of those who would transgress against us; we all stand in readiness to defend our families, our homes and our country. We will defend it with our blood and soul and meager resources.

We ask ALLAH to protect us from this impending evil, to give us peace and protect our souls. Our people have not transgressed against the people of America. We pray for our suffering to end.

Thank you brother for asking about our concerns, thank you for giving us a voice. Thank you for taking the risk necessary for truth and justice to be heard. Express our gratitude to everyone who supports our cause. Thank the Muslim, Christian and Jewish people in America and all people that support us.

Your brother, Osama Saad

After my inquiry in early October 2002, I received this message from a relative in Iraq, who is anxious about the fate of elderly aunts who he cares for. He feels the beat of the war drum. Do we feel the beat of their hearts?

from the records, Ali-Salaam

Beware the leader who bangs the drums of war in order to whip the citizenry into a patriotic fervor, for patriotism is indeed a double-edged sword. It both emboldens the blood, just as it narrows the mind. And when the drums of war have reached a fever pitch and the blood boils with hate and the mind has closed, the leader will have no need in seizing the rights of the citizenry. Rather, the citizenry, infused with fear and blinded by patriotism, will offer up all of their rights unto the leader and gladly so. How do I know? For this is what I have done. And I am Caesar.

Julius Caesar

Epilogue

Becoming human is to integrate kindness and courage into an ethical character with moral values.

Being human is to express our inherent spiritual nobility in the ordinary events of everyday life; breath by breath, moment by moment.

from the records, Ali-Salaam

~ believe...and do good works ~

Request Ali-Salaam to speak at your event
email: **info** @ ali-salaam.com

" By the token of time (passing of the ages) Verily Mankind is at loss, except those who believe; and that do good works, who enjoin one another in the mutual teaching of truth and are steadfast and patient."
The Qur'an, Sura 103

ISBN 1-55395015-1
9 781553 950158